ANTICIPATION FOR SPAIN

Unlocking Maximum Anticipation

Michael Kißling

Transparency is important to me

As an independent author, I handle every step - from the first rough draft to the final design - on my own and with great passion. To bring this book to life, **I used paid AI tools**. Not out of convenience, but because AI-generated images have become remarkably beautiful, and the AI reliably catches all my spelling mistakes and missing letters.

I'm always looking to improve my content. I'm open to suggestions and constructive feedback! Feel free to send them to the email address you'll find on the last page. I promise to check my inbox regularly - at least once a week.

And of course, one thing must not be missed... I can't even begin to tell you how incredibly happy every single positive review you leave on Amazon makes me. It's like a little gift to me and my very own anticipation and motivation for the next book!

The Magic of Anticipation

Anticipation is a powerful and joyful emotion that transforms waiting into a meaningful experience. It begins the moment you decide to take a trip and lasts well beyond your return, enriching your life with excitement, purpose, and inspiration. When looking forward to a vacation, such as one to Spain, anticipation brings happiness by releasing dopamine, the brain's "feel-good" chemical, creating a positive outlook long before the trip begins.

Anticipation fosters a sense of purpose, turning preparation into a rewarding part of the journey. Activities like planning, packing, or learning about your destination provide a sense of accomplishment and make each step of the process exciting. Visualization adds another layer, allowing you to mentally experience moments like strolling through Barcelona's lively streets or unwinding on a terrace overlooking the Mediterranean. These imagined experiences enhance your connection to the trip and boost overall well-being.

Incorporating small rituals, such as marking off days on a calendar or enjoying Spanish-inspired activities at home, further heightens the sense of anticipation. Sharing these moments with family or friends strengthens relationships and turns the countdown into a cherished part of the journey. Even unexpected challenges during the trip preparation can lead to creative solutions and personal growth.

Anticipation teaches the value of living in the present while looking forward to the future. It transforms preparation into a joyful extension of the vacation itself. This mindset encourages optimism, enriches daily life, and makes every moment leading up to the trip as fulfilling as the journey itself. By embracing the art of anticipation, you set the stage for a memorable and deeply rewarding travel experience.

Contents

How This Book Works...

...we'll reveal the magic formula right away.

1.

This book is your smart companion, bringing you closer to the perfect vacation vibe with every page. Our goal? Maximum anticipation! The best part: there are no rules. Simply read whatever you feel like and start wherever you want. Some sections might feel a bit similar - and that's entirely intentional. With purposeful repetition, your excitement grows wonderfully, and each time, the butterflies in your stomach will get just a little bigger.

2.

In this book, you will find exclusively black-and-white images - and for a very specific reason: They spark your imagination and leave room for the unknown. Perhaps you've seen this in fairy tale movies, where a black-and-white image comes to life just before the scene unfolds. That's exactly how it should be for you: The colors will reveal their full brilliance only when you actually experience your vacation. A small psychological trick to heighten your anticipation, which is also more environmentally friendly than glossy color prints!

From Daydream to Departure

Shaping Your Spanish Getaway

There is a magical moment when a dream begins to take shape, transitioning from a fleeting thought into something tangible. The moment you decide that Spain is your next destination, anticipation starts bubbling up inside you. But excitement alone won't get you there. Turning that dream into a well-crafted plan is what truly brings the journey to life. It is not about rigid schedules or overwhelming to-do lists. It is about channeling your enthusiasm into something productive, ensuring that every detail adds to the joy of looking forward to your trip.

The Art of Early Planning

The best trips don't just happen. They are built layer by layer, with each new discovery adding to the excitement. The earlier you start preparing, the more rewarding the process becomes. Booking flights and accommodations in advance not only saves money but also gives you a sense of security. Once those essentials are in place, the adventure truly begins. Researching destinations, imagining yourself wandering through narrow cobbled streets or basking under the Mediterranean sun, fills the weeks leading up to departure with anticipation.

One of the most effective ways to fuel this excitement is to keep a dedicated travel notebook or digital journal. This becomes the place where ideas take shape, from must-visit spots to personal goals for the trip. Spain is a country of contrasts, from the vibrant energy of Barcelona to the tranquil white villages of Andalusia. Jotting down what appeals to you most helps narrow your focus, ensuring that your trip aligns with your personal vision. Some travelers crave the thrill of exploring bustling city life, while others long for a peaceful retreat by the sea. By writing down these preferences, you begin to mold your journey into something uniquely yours.

Shaping the Experience to Your Desires

A trip to Spain is more than a getaway. It is an experience that can be tailored to your deepest wishes. The key is to identify what truly excites you. Do you dream of long, slow mornings at a sun-drenched café, sipping café con leche and watching the world go by? Or is your heart set on hiking rugged coastal paths, feeling the salty breeze against your skin? Perhaps your imagination is captivated by Spanish history, and you can already picture yourself standing in the shadow of the Alhambra, tracing your fingers along the intricate carvings of centuries past.

These are not just vague ideas; they are the core of what will make your trip meaningful. Writing them down is not only about making a list. It is about engaging with your emotions, allowing yourself to feel the thrill of what awaits. The simple act of visualizing these experiences intensifies your anticipation, making every passing day feel like a step closer to something extraordinary.

The Motivation Hidden in the Details

Some people see planning as a chore, but in reality, it is an opportunity to deepen your connection to your upcoming adventure. The more time you spend immersing yourself in Spain's culture, the richer your experience will be. Imagine the delight of arriving at a bustling tapas bar in Madrid and already knowing the difference between a ración and a pincho. Imagine stepping into a flamenco show in Seville, recognizing the rhythms and emotions of the performance because you took the time to learn about this passionate art form beforehand.

Every small effort you make now will amplify your experience later. Learning a few essential Spanish phrases, reading about local customs, or even watching Spanish films to absorb the atmosphere—all of these things add layers to your anticipation. They transform your trip from something distant and abstract into something you are actively preparing for. Instead of counting down the days with impatience, you fill them with excitement and purpose.

A Balance Between Structure and Spontaneity

One of the greatest challenges in planning a trip is finding the right balance between structure and freedom. It is tempting to map out every detail, ensuring that no opportunity is missed. Yet, some of the most memorable moments happen when you leave space for spontaneity. The key is to set a flexible framework—an outline of what you most want to experience—without restricting yourself to a rigid schedule.

Think of your plan as a canvas rather than a blueprint. Highlight key locations you want to visit, but leave room for unexpected discoveries. If you stumble upon a charming local festival or find yourself lost in conversation with a friendly shopkeeper, you will want the freedom to embrace these moments rather than feeling bound by a tight itinerary. Spain has a way of surprising its visitors, offering hidden treasures when you least expect them.

Embracing the Waiting Period as Part of the Journey

The weeks or months before a trip can sometimes feel like an eternity, but in reality, they are an essential part of the experience. This is the time to savor the build-up, to let the anticipation grow. Travel is not just about the destination. It is about the journey, and that journey begins long before you step on a plane.

Engage with the culture in small ways. Try cooking a traditional Spanish dish, like patatas bravas or tortilla de patatas, to bring a taste of Spain into your home. Listen to Spanish music, letting the rhythms of flamenco or the melodies of Spanish guitar transport you mentally to another place. Read novels set in Spain, allowing your imagination to wander through its landscapes. Each of these activities deepens your excitement, making you feel as if your journey has already begun.

Packing as a Ritual of Anticipation

Even something as practical as packing can become a source of joy when approached with the right mindset. Instead of leaving it to the last minute, turn it into a ritual that marks the final step of preparation. Choosing the right clothes for Spanish weather, selecting a comfortable pair of walking shoes, and setting aside a special notebook for travel reflections—these small acts solidify the reality of your trip.

Packing thoughtfully also ensures that you bring only what enhances your experience. A lightweight scarf can serve as both a fashion statement and a practical shield against the strong Spanish sun. A reusable water bottle keeps you hydrated as you explore. A pocket-sized Spanish phrasebook can become your best friend in moments when words fail you. Each item in your suitcase should contribute to the smoothness and enjoyment of your journey.

The Power of a Countdown

Marking the days until departure adds to the sense of excitement. Whether it is a calendar on your wall or a digital countdown on your phone, seeing the number of days shrink makes the trip feel more real. Some travelers enjoy setting small milestones along the way, such as trying a new Spanish dish each week or watching a travel documentary about Spain. These rituals keep the excitement alive, ensuring that anticipation remains a joyful experience rather than an impatient longing.

By embracing every stage of the planning process, you transform waiting into an active part of your journey. The trip itself will be incredible, but the time leading up to it holds its own magic. Every step you take now, every small detail you consider, builds toward something unforgettable. The dream has already begun to take form. Soon, it will be reality.

Spain is Europe's sun oasis

- whether on the beach, in the mountains, or in the cities,

the sun follows you everywhere.

Discovering Spain

…before You Arrive

A journey begins long before you step off a plane or unpack your suitcase in a hotel room. The best way to truly savor the anticipation of an upcoming trip is to immerse yourself in your destination before you even get there. Spain, with its rich tapestry of history, culture, and diverse landscapes, offers endless opportunities to explore from a distance. The more you familiarize yourself with the places, people, and language in advance, the more rewarding your visit will be. Every bit of knowledge adds to the excitement, turning the unfamiliar into something that already feels like home.

Walking the Streets Before You Arrive

One of the greatest advantages of modern travel preparation is the ability to explore a place without setting foot on its soil. Technology allows you to roam the narrow alleys of Seville, stroll through Barcelona's vibrant markets, or admire Madrid's grand boulevards—all from the comfort of your home. Google Maps and its Street View function are invaluable tools for this. They give you the ability to "walk" down the very streets you will soon be exploring, getting a sense of the layout, the atmosphere, and the hidden corners you might not have noticed otherwise.

By zooming in on different neighborhoods, you can identify cafés where you might want to enjoy your morning coffee, boutique shops that catch your interest, or quiet plazas perfect for a moment of rest. Exploring these areas in advance helps you develop a sense of familiarity, making your arrival in Spain feel less like stepping into the unknown and more like returning to a place you have already begun to love. This kind of preparation does not take away from the thrill of discovery. Instead, it deepens it, allowing you to look forward to specific experiences rather than feeling overwhelmed by too many choices at once.

The Power of a Virtual Visit

Beyond maps, there are countless ways to virtually experience Spain before you arrive. Many museums, historical sites, and cultural institutions offer virtual tours. Imagine stepping inside the halls of the Prado Museum, admiring works by Velázquez and Goya, long before you ever stand in front of them in person. Walking through the Alhambra in a digital format before visiting in real life allows you to appreciate its details more fully when you finally see its intricate carvings and stunning gardens. Live webcams placed in major cities let you witness the energy of Spain in real-time. Watching the waves crash against the beaches of San Sebastián or seeing the crowds meander through Plaza Mayor in Madrid gives you a small taste of what awaits. These glimpses serve as tiny windows into the daily rhythm of life, feeding your imagination and making the wait for your trip all the more exciting.

Tuning into the Sounds of Spain

A destination is not just about what you see but also about what you hear. The sounds of Spain—lively conversations spilling from cafés, the distant strumming of a flamenco guitar, the rhythmic clatter of tapas plates being set on a bar—are just as much a part of the experience as the sights. By incorporating Spanish music into your daily life, you allow yourself to mentally transport to your destination before you even board a plane.

Flamenco, with its deep, emotional intensity, offers a glimpse into the soul of Spain. Listening to artists like Paco de Lucía or Camarón de la Isla introduces you to the expressive beauty of this art form. If modern music is more your style, Spanish pop, rock, and indie bands provide another avenue to connect with the country's culture. Even tuning in to Spanish radio stations or podcasts immerses you in the language and rhythm of daily life, making the transition to being there feel seamless.

Bringing Spain to Your Taste Buds

Food is one of the most powerful ways to connect with a culture, and Spain's cuisine is legendary. Preparing traditional Spanish dishes at home is a sensory way to engage with your destination in advance. The process of cooking Spanish food—whether it is the slow stirring of a saffron-laced paella, the crisping of golden churros in hot oil, or the layering of a simple yet delicious tortilla de patatas—creates a direct link between you and the country you are about to visit.

Each dish tells a story. Sipping a glass of Rioja while reading about Spain's wine regions makes the experience richer. Trying your hand at homemade gazpacho transports you to the warm southern coast. Experimenting with Spanish ingredients like smoked paprika, sherry vinegar, or Iberian ham adds layers of depth to your appreciation of the flavors you will soon experience firsthand. By the time you arrive, you will not just be tasting Spanish food. You will be recognizing it, appreciating its nuances, and understanding its cultural significance.

Learning the Language, One Phrase at a Time

Even if you are not fluent in Spanish, knowing a few essential phrases before your trip transforms the experience. The beauty of learning some of the language is not just in practical communication but in the connection it creates with locals. A simple **"Buenos días"** at a bakery or a **"Gracias"** after receiving your café con leche goes a long way in showing respect and appreciation for the culture.

Instead of attempting to memorize endless vocabulary lists, focus on phrases that you will actually use. Greetings, polite expressions, and ordering food are excellent starting points. Watching Spanish films or TV shows with subtitles helps you absorb pronunciation and rhythm naturally. Reading simple texts in Spanish, even children's books or travel blogs, familiarizes you with common words and expressions.

Many language apps provide bite-sized lessons, making it easy to practice a few minutes a day. The key is not to aim for perfection but to build confidence in using what you know. Locals always appreciate the effort, even if your grammar is not flawless. The reward is in the smiles and friendly responses you receive, which make you feel more connected to the place and its people.

Understanding Cultural Nuances

Every country has unspoken social norms and customs that shape daily interactions. In Spain, knowing these small details enhances your ability to blend in and feel at ease. The Spanish way of life is famously relaxed, with long lunch breaks, late dinners, and an emphasis on enjoying the moment. Understanding this rhythm in advance helps you embrace it rather than feeling out of sync.

For instance, meal times are significantly later than in many other countries. Lunch, the largest meal of the day, often takes place around 2 or 3 PM, while dinner rarely starts before 9 PM. Tipping culture is different as well, with small change left for good service rather than the percentage-based system found elsewhere. Greetings often involve a light kiss on both cheeks rather than a handshake, especially in social settings.

Taking the time to learn these small but meaningful aspects of Spanish life deepens your appreciation for the culture. It allows you to move through your trip with greater ease, making you feel more like a participant rather than just an observer.

Letting Your Imagination Lead the Way

The beauty of anticipation is that it gives you the freedom to dream without limits. As you explore Spain from afar, let your imagination take over. Picture yourself watching the sunset over the rooftops of Granada, standing in the cool shade of a palm-lined plaza, or feeling the sea breeze as you walk along a coastal promenade. These visions are not just daydreams. They are stepping stones toward an experience that is waiting for you.

Every small action you take now—whether it is listening to Spanish music, practicing a few key phrases, or mapping out your ideal morning walk—makes the destination feel closer. By the time you set foot in Spain, you will not be arriving in an unfamiliar place. You will be stepping into a world you have already begun to know and love.

Spain impresses with over 4.964 kilometers of coastline, offering picturesque sandy beaches and hidden coves.

Embracing the Heartbeat of Spain

Culture and Knowledge

To visit Spain is to immerse yourself in a culture that pulses with energy, vibrancy, and a rich tapestry of history. Each region of this sun-drenched country has its own unique character, shaped by centuries of tradition, conquest, and creativity. From the architectural wonders of the Moors to the fervor of flamenco, Spain's cultural wealth is a treasure trove waiting to be discovered. By delving into the nation's heritage, customs, and everyday life, your anticipation grows richer, as if you are not just planning a trip but preparing to step into a living story.

Historical Footprints Across Centuries

The history of Spain is a captivating saga of empires, battles, and cultural exchange. It is a land where the legacies of the Romans, Visigoths, Moors, and Catholic monarchs intertwine, leaving an indelible mark on the landscape and its people. The Roman aqueducts of Segovia, still standing after nearly two millennia, whisper tales of ancient engineering prowess. In Córdoba, the majestic arches of the Mezquita showcase the artistic brilliance of the Islamic Golden Age, while the imposing cathedrals of Seville and Toledo reflect the grandeur of the Spanish Reconquista.

Understanding these historical layers enriches your experience. Walking through the Alhambra's gardens, you are not merely admiring its beauty but also grasping the intricate blend of Islamic art and Christian influence that defines Spain's unique aesthetic. Visiting the hauntingly beautiful Sagrada Família in Barcelona becomes more profound when you know it is the unfinished masterpiece of Antoni Gaudí, a visionary who sought to blend nature with architecture.

Each region has its own story to tell. Galicia, with its lush green landscapes and rugged coastlines, carries the mystique of Celtic traditions and the spiritual allure of the Camino de Santiago. In the Basque Country, the tension between cultural preservation and modern identity adds depth to the vibrant city of Bilbao and its world-famous Guggenheim Museum. Andalusia's white-washed villages and passionate flamenco rhythms evoke memories of a Moorish past and a relentless spirit of artistic expression.

The Rhythm of Spanish Life

Spanish culture is perhaps best known for its zest for life, a quality embodied in its daily rituals and social customs. The concept of **"la sobremesa,"** the leisurely time spent lingering over a meal, talking, and savoring each other's company, is central to Spanish hospitality. Unlike the rushed meals of other cultures, Spaniards take pride in enjoying their food and the conversations that accompany it. Dining out is as much about community as it is about sustenance, and tapas culture perfectly encapsulates this. Small plates meant for sharing encourage connection, inviting you to sample a variety of flavors while engaging in lively discussions. Siesta, though often misunderstood, reflects Spain's deep appreciation for balance and well-being. In many parts of the country, particularly smaller towns and rural areas, the afternoon pause is a sacred tradition. Shops close, streets grow quiet, and families retreat from the heat to rest. It is a reminder that life need not be hurried, that moments of rest are as valuable as those of productivity. Embracing this slower pace, even temporarily, offers a refreshing contrast to the frenetic energy of modern life.

The Spanish timetable itself is a cultural experience. Mornings begin with a light **"desayuno"** of coffee and a small pastry. Lunch, the largest meal of the day, takes place in the mid-afternoon, followed by a late dinner often stretching past 9 PM. The nightlife is equally distinct. Spaniards are known for their **"marcha,"** the ability to enjoy long nights filled with music, dancing, and socializing, whether at a local bar or a bustling city plaza.

Traditions That Shape Identity

Spain's calendar is dotted with festivals that offer insight into its soul. From the explosive energy of **Las Fallas** in Valencia, where towering effigies are set ablaze, to the solemn processions of **Semana Santa** in Seville, each celebration tells a story of faith, community, and artistic expression. **La Tomatina** in Buñol, a chaotic tomato-throwing festival, contrasts sharply with the elegance of **Feria de Abril** in Seville, where locals don traditional attire and dance **Sevillanas** until dawn.

Even smaller traditions carry significant weight. In Catalonia, **La Diada de Sant Jordi** combines the exchange of books and roses, celebrating both love and literature. The **Castellers** of Catalonia, who form human towers, embody the region's spirit of unity and perseverance. In Galicia, the haunting notes of the **gaita** (bagpipe) and the mystical rituals of **Noite Meiga** (Night of the Witches) speak to an ancient Celtic heritage.

Artistic Expressions of a Diverse Nation

Art in Spain is not confined to museums and galleries; it permeates daily life. The works of Spanish masters like **Pablo Picasso, Salvador Dalí,** and **Francisco Goya** are revered worldwide, yet their influence extends beyond canvas and sculpture. Picasso's birthplace in Málaga offers a glimpse into the formative years of a genius who redefined modern art. Dalí's surreal landscapes, inspired by the rugged beauty of Catalonia, challenge viewers to question reality itself. Goya's powerful depictions of war and society, preserved in Madrid's Prado Museum, remain as poignant today as when they were first painted.

Flamenco, more than just a dance, is a visceral expression of emotion that combines music, movement, and storytelling. Originating in Andalusia, its rhythms and melodies carry the echoes of Romani, Moorish, and Jewish traditions. Whether performed in a grand theatre or an intimate **"tablao,"** flamenco is a mesmerizing blend of passion, melancholy, and defiance. Participating in a flamenco class or simply watching a live performance deepens your understanding of Spain's complex cultural fabric. Spanish craftsmanship also deserves recognition. From the intricate **damascene** metalwork of Toledo to the vibrant ceramics of Talavera de la Reina, artisans continue age-old traditions with pride. The textile crafts of Galicia, the leatherwork of Ubrique, and the intricate lace of Almagro are tangible connections to Spain's artisanal heritage. Bringing home a handmade souvenir is not just a keepsake. It is a piece of history, crafted by hands that continue to honor the past while adapting to the present.

Connecting Through Language and Gesture

Language is a bridge to understanding a culture's values and worldview. While Castilian Spanish is the official language, Spain's linguistic diversity reflects its regional identities. Catalan, Basque, and Galician are spoken in their respective regions, each with its own history and cultural significance. Learning even a few words in these languages demonstrates respect and curiosity, fostering a deeper connection with locals.

Body language and gestures are equally important in Spain. A warm embrace, a kiss on each cheek, or an enthusiastic pat on the back are common forms of greeting, reflecting the country's open and affectionate nature. The famed Spanish **"olé"** is not just an exclamation; it is a verbal applause, a way of expressing admiration and encouragement. Understanding these subtleties enriches interactions, making every encounter more meaningful and memorable.

Daily Life and the Spanish Outlook

At its core, Spanish culture is about embracing life with open arms. Family is the cornerstone of society, and gatherings are frequent, lively affairs filled with laughter, debate, and shared meals. Sundays are often reserved for family time, whether it is a leisurely lunch at a countryside **"venta"** or a stroll through a local park.

Spaniards value community, and neighborhoods function as extended families. The local **"barrio"** is more than just a place to live. It is a social hub where everyone from shopkeepers to children plays a role in daily life. Markets are vibrant centers of interaction, where bargaining over fresh produce becomes an opportunity for conversation and connection.

Through exploring Spain's history, traditions, and daily life, your anticipation transforms into a deeper appreciation. The trip becomes not just a visit to a foreign land but a journey into the heart of a culture that values passion, creativity, and community above all else. By immersing yourself in Spain's rich heritage, you prepare to experience it not as a tourist but as a welcomed guest, ready to participate in the timeless dance of Spanish life.

With more than 300 radiant sunny days a year,

Spain promises boundless warmth

and pure vacation magic.

Unforgettable Journeys

...through Spain's Wonders

Spain is a country where every corner holds a story, every landscape invites adventure, and every city or village offers a unique glimpse into its vibrant culture. Whether you are drawn to breathtaking natural wonders, historic landmarks, or hidden gems off the beaten path, the possibilities for excursions are endless. The beauty of exploring Spain lies in its diversity. From towering mountains and sun-drenched coastlines to medieval towns and architectural masterpieces, the country invites travelers to immerse themselves in unforgettable experiences.

The Timeless Allure of Spain's Cities

Each of Spain's major cities has its own distinct charm, making them must-visit destinations for any traveler. Madrid, the pulsating heart of the country, blends grandeur with a lively modern spirit. Strolling through the elegant Plaza Mayor, you can almost hear the echoes of historical gatherings, while the majestic Royal Palace stands as a testament to Spain's regal past. Art lovers will find their paradise in the world-famous Prado Museum, where works by Goya, Velázquez, and El Greco transport visitors through centuries of artistic mastery. Just a short train ride away, the ancient city of Toledo offers a mesmerizing fusion of Christian, Jewish, and Islamic influences, with its labyrinthine streets and awe-inspiring cathedral.

Barcelona, in contrast, is a city of imagination and bold expression. The architectural genius of Antoni Gaudí is everywhere, from the surreal curves of Casa Batlló to the otherworldly grandeur of the still-unfinished Sagrada Família. A walk along La Rambla immerses you in the city's vibrant street life, while the Gothic Quarter reveals layers of medieval history at every turn. For a panoramic view of the city, a hike up to Park Güell offers a dazzling display of color, mosaics, and whimsical design.

Seville, the sun-drenched jewel of Andalusia, seduces visitors with its intoxicating blend of Moorish and Spanish influences. The city's soul is found in its flamenco tablaos, where passionate dancers and musicians bring this ancient art form to life. The Alcázar, a stunning palace complex with intricate Islamic-style architecture, transports visitors to a time when sultans and kings ruled over this land. At sunset, the sight of the illuminated Giralda tower and the vast Plaza de España makes it clear why Seville is considered one of the most romantic cities in Spain.

Natural Wonders and Scenic Escapes

Beyond the bustling cities, Spain's natural landscapes offer some of the most breathtaking excursions in Europe. The Picos de Europa, a mountain range in the north, provides a striking contrast to Spain's sun-soaked image. Towering peaks, deep gorges, and emerald-green valleys make this an ideal destination for hiking, wildlife spotting, and exploring picturesque villages like Potes, where traditional stone houses and cozy taverns welcome visitors with warm hospitality.

For those drawn to coastal beauty, the rugged Costa Brava in Catalonia is a dreamlike escape. Its hidden coves, crystal-clear waters, and charming fishing villages such as Cadaqués and Calella de Palafrugell provide a serene retreat from the larger tourist hotspots. The wild landscapes of Cabo de Gata in Almería, with its volcanic rock formations and untouched beaches, offer an entirely different experience—one that feels like stepping into an undiscovered paradise.

Spain's islands also promise extraordinary excursions. Mallorca, the largest of the Balearics, enchants with its dramatic cliffs, secluded beaches, and mountain villages like Valldemossa, where composer Frédéric Chopin once sought inspiration. Meanwhile, Lanzarote in the Canary Islands stuns with its lunar landscapes, shaped by volcanic eruptions and preserved within the otherworldly Timanfaya National Park. Exploring these islands allows travelers to experience Spain's astonishing variety of natural wonders.

Journeying Through History and Tradition

For those who crave a deeper connection with Spain's past, the country offers countless historical excursions that bring history to life. One of the most awe-inspiring destinations is the Alhambra in Granada, a palace-city where Moorish rulers once resided in unparalleled splendor. Wandering through its intricate courtyards, admiring the delicate stucco work and the poetic inscriptions on the walls, one cannot help but feel transported to another time. The surrounding Albaicín district, with its whitewashed houses and winding streets, offers a glimpse into the city's medieval past and a spectacular viewpoint over the Alhambra itself.

Another unmissable experience is the Camino de Santiago, the legendary pilgrimage route that leads to the grand cathedral in Santiago de Compostela. Whether walking a short section or undertaking the full journey, the Camino offers a sense of introspection and camaraderie among fellow travelers. The landscapes shift from rolling vineyards to misty Galician forests, making every step a part of the spiritual and cultural tapestry woven into this path.

Southern Spain also holds treasures such as Ronda, a dramatic cliffside town where an ancient bridge spans a deep gorge, offering breathtaking views. Ronda's bullring, one of the oldest in Spain, provides insight into the country's deeply ingrained traditions. Meanwhile, the city of Córdoba, once the capital of Islamic Spain, invites visitors to marvel at the grandeur of the Mezquita, a mosque-turned-cathedral whose endless columns and red-and-white arches create an almost hypnotic effect.

Culinary Pilgrimages and Local Flavors

Spain is a paradise for food lovers, and embarking on a culinary journey is one of the best ways to experience its regions. San Sebastián, in the Basque Country, is a must-visit for its renowned pintxos—bite-sized delicacies served in the city's lively bars. Here, hopping from one tavern to the next is a way of life, with each stop offering a new explosion of flavors, from seafood delights to rich Iberian ham. In La Rioja, Spain's most famous wine region, a visit to a bodega offers the opportunity to sip world-class vintages while gazing out at endless vineyards. Many wineries offer guided tastings, allowing visitors to appreciate the nuances of different Tempranillo blends. In Jerez de la Frontera, sherry takes center stage, and a tour of the town's historic cellars reveals the art of aging this fortified wine, often accompanied by a traditional flamenco performance.

For those who wish to explore Spain's culinary traditions at a deeper level, a trip to a local food market is an essential experience. Barcelona's Boqueria, Madrid's Mercado de San Miguel, and Valencia's Mercado Central burst with color, aromas, and the hum of daily life. Sampling fresh seafood, artisanal cheeses, or churros dipped in thick chocolate connects travelers to the flavors that define Spanish cuisine.

Off the Beaten Path: Hidden Gems Worth Discovering

Beyond the well-known attractions, Spain hides countless lesser-known destinations that are equally captivating. Albarracín, a medieval village nestled in the mountains of Aragón, feels like a place frozen in time, with its pink-hued walls and winding stone streets. In Extremadura, the city of Cáceres showcases a remarkably well-preserved medieval quarter, where wandering through its quiet alleys is like stepping into a different century. For those who seek artistic inspiration, the town of Figueres in Catalonia is home to the Dalí Theatre-Museum, a surrealist masterpiece designed by the artist himself. Every room offers a glimpse into Dalí's eccentric mind, making it one of the most unique museums in the world. In contrast, the windmills of Consuegra in Castilla-La Mancha bring literature to life, evoking the legendary journey of Don Quixote as he mistook them for giants in Cervantes' classic novel.

Spain's treasures are endless, each excursion offering a new dimension of discovery. Whether marveling at grand palaces, hiking along coastal cliffs, tasting the bold flavors of regional cuisine, or wandering through forgotten villages, every journey deepens the anticipation and excitement for the adventure ahead. The true magic of Spain lies not just in seeing these wonders but in experiencing them, in feeling their stories unfold as you become part of the landscape.

The sunsets in Spain bathe the sea

and landscape in a magical golden light.

The Journey Begins in Your Mind

A dream journey

The excitement of an upcoming trip does not begin when you step onto a plane or set foot in a new city. It starts in the imagination, in those quiet moments when you close your eyes and picture yourself arriving in Spain, feeling the warm breeze against your skin, hearing the distant chatter of a café, and inhaling the unmistakable scent of the sea or citrus groves. Long before you pack your bags, your journey has already begun. It unfolds in your thoughts, shaping your expectations, heightening your anticipation, and making every passing day feel like a step closer to a dream turning into reality.

Envisioning the Moment of Arrival

Picture yourself on the plane, the anticipation building as the captain announces the descent into Spain. The hum of conversation rises as passengers stir in their seats, peering through the windows to catch their first glimpse of the landscape below. Maybe it is the golden coastline of Barcelona stretching endlessly into the horizon, the sun-drenched hills of Andalusia rolling gently beneath you, or the towering peaks of the Pyrenees marking the border between Spain and France. You are almost there.

The wheels touch the ground, and as the plane slows, a rush of excitement floods through you. You step into the terminal, a place buzzing with life. The scent of fresh espresso and baked pastries drifts through the air from a nearby café. Travelers bustle past, speaking in Spanish, their words a melody of soft consonants and rolling vowels. There is something electrifying about this moment, the first few minutes in a new country where every sound, every sight, every smell feels heightened, carrying the thrill of discovery.

As you collect your luggage and step outside, the warmth of the Spanish sun greets you. The sky is a brilliant blue, the air rich with the scent of orange blossoms or the salty tang of the sea, depending on your destination. A taxi or train awaits, ready to take you into the heart of the city or along winding roads that lead to charming villages. Every detail feels fresh and exhilarating. You have arrived, and the adventure is yours to shape.

Imagining the Perfect Vacation Day

From the moment you wake up in Spain, time moves differently. There is no rush, no need to check endless notifications or dive into obligations. Instead, you open your eyes to soft morning light filtering through the curtains, stretching lazily as you listen to the distant sounds of a city waking up or the gentle rhythm of waves against the shore. The air is warm, carrying the scent of freshly baked bread and brewing coffee from a café nearby.

A perfect morning begins with a slow walk through the quiet streets, stopping at a local bakery for a flaky croissant or a slice of traditional Spanish toast topped with crushed tomatoes and olive oil. The first sip of café con leche feels like an embrace, smooth and rich, warming you from the inside out. Locals chat at neighboring tables, exchanging laughter and greetings, their relaxed demeanor reminding you that here, life is meant to be savored.

Mid-morning invites exploration. Perhaps you find yourself wandering through the intricate alleys of a medieval quarter, each turn revealing hidden courtyards with blooming bougainvillea and the faint trickle of an old stone fountain. Maybe you have chosen a coastal retreat, where the ocean calls you to dip your toes into its cool embrace, the sun warming your back as fishing boats bob gently in the harbor.

Lunch is an experience in itself, unhurried and indulgent. You settle into a sunlit terrace, ordering a spread of tapas—crispy patatas bravas drizzled in a smoky sauce, delicate slices of jamón ibérico that melt on your tongue, and freshly grilled seafood that tastes of the sea. The world slows down as you sip a chilled glass of local wine, the conversation flowing effortlessly with friends or newfound acquaintances.

The afternoon stretches before you like an open canvas. Perhaps you visit an art museum, standing before a Picasso or Dalí, feeling the energy of their brushstrokes resonate through time. Or maybe you choose a quiet siesta in the shade of a palm tree, the sounds of Spain lulling you into peaceful rest.

As evening approaches, the golden hour bathes the streets in a warm glow. You find yourself drawn to a lively plaza, where musicians strum guitars and couples sway in impromptu dances. Dinner is a slow affair, beginning late, as is tradition, with plates of paella shared among friends, the saffron-infused rice perfectly tender, the seafood glistening in the candlelight.

Nightfall in Spain holds its own magic. You stroll through the streets, feeling the cool air against your skin, passing by open-air bars where laughter and music spill into the night. A final stop at a rooftop terrace grants you a breathtaking view—a sea of twinkling lights stretching toward the horizon, the city alive with possibility. This is Spain at its finest. This is the dream you are about to live.

The Power of Mental Travel

The mind is a powerful tool, capable of transporting you anywhere long before your physical journey begins. Visualization techniques, often used in sports psychology and mindfulness practices, allow you to experience your upcoming adventure in vivid detail, reinforcing excitement and deepening your emotional connection to your destination.

By setting aside a few minutes each day to close your eyes and imagine yourself in Spain, you cultivate a sense of familiarity and comfort with your journey. Picture yourself navigating the streets confidently, ordering food effortlessly, and engaging with locals warmly. The more you visualize these moments, the more natural they will feel when they finally unfold in real life.

Another technique to enhance anticipation is autogenic training, a relaxation method that uses guided imagery to create a state of deep calm and mental clarity. Sitting in a quiet space, you focus on slow, steady breathing, allowing tension to melt away. With each breath, you imagine yourself stepping further into your journey—feeling the cobblestone streets beneath your feet, hearing the distant sounds of a Spanish guitar, tasting the sweetness of a ripe fig plucked from a market stall. These sensory details anchor you in the experience, making your trip feel not like a distant event but an unfolding reality.

Turning Anticipation into a Daily Ritual

Anticipation is a gift, a way to stretch the joy of travel far beyond the days you will physically spend in Spain. By weaving small rituals into your daily life, you can bring the spirit of your upcoming journey into the present. Cooking Spanish dishes at home, listening to flamenco or Spanish guitar music, reading novels set in Spain, or even changing your phone's language settings to Spanish are all ways to bridge the gap between now and departure.

Each time you engage with something connected to Spain, your excitement is renewed. Even marking off days on a calendar or keeping a travel journal filled with thoughts, sketches, or notes about places you wish to visit enhances the experience. Rather than impatiently waiting for the trip to begin, you actively participate in its buildup, making every moment leading up to it just as meaningful as the trip itself.

Stepping into the Dream

When the long-awaited day finally arrives, and you step onto that plane, it will not feel like the beginning of something unknown. It will feel like stepping into a world you have already come to know and love. The sights, sounds, and tastes you imagined will now unfold before you in real-time, richer and more vivid than you ever could have anticipated.

A journey does not begin at the airport. It begins in the heart and mind, in the quiet moments of longing, in the excitement of preparation, in the way you allow yourself to dream. The magic of Spain is already within you, waiting to be lived. And soon, you will not just be dreaming of your perfect day—you will be living it.

In Spain, the feeling of boundless freedom merges with Mediterranean flair and a perfect blend of relaxation and adventure.

Preparing Yourself for the Journey

Your personal goals until the vacation

A vacation does not begin the moment you leave your home. It starts long before that, in the days and weeks leading up to your departure. The anticipation is not only about packing a suitcase or checking off a to-do list. It is about mentally and physically preparing yourself to step into the adventure fully present, energized, and free from lingering worries. Setting personal goals before your vacation ensures that you arrive in Spain not just as a visitor but as someone ready to embrace every moment.

Organizing Life Before Departure

Before setting off on your journey, there is a certain satisfaction in knowing that everything at home is in order. Taking care of unfinished tasks, both big and small, ensures that you leave with a clear mind, unburdened by worries that might otherwise creep into your time away. Bills should be scheduled, work responsibilities wrapped up, and any household matters arranged so that nothing lingers in the back of your mind while you are sipping a café con leche in a sunlit plaza.

Checking travel documents early is a simple but essential task. A passport nearing expiration, a forgotten visa requirement, or an expired driver's license could become a last-minute stressor. Ensuring that these details are handled well in advance provides peace of mind. Likewise, securing travel insurance, making copies of important documents, and organizing digital backups of necessary information are all small steps that create a seamless travel experience.

Beyond paperwork, preparing your home for your absence adds to the sense of ease. Arranging for a neighbor to collect mail, setting up automatic light timers, or even doing a final deep clean before leaving makes returning home much more pleasant. There is something deeply comforting about knowing that everything is in place, allowing you to focus entirely on the experience ahead.

Enhancing Health and Well-Being

A vacation is a time to feel your best, to walk for miles through winding streets, to swim in the sea, to dance under the stars, and to indulge in local flavors without hesitation. Preparing your body for this adventure enhances the experience, ensuring that fatigue or discomfort does not hold you back from embracing every opportunity.

Physical preparation does not mean extreme changes or unrealistic goals. It is about small, intentional steps to boost energy and endurance. If long city walks or hiking excursions are on the itinerary, gradually increasing daily movement before the trip can make a noticeable difference. Taking the stairs instead of the elevator, going for longer walks, or engaging in light strength exercises helps build stamina. Not only does this make exploration more enjoyable, but it also reduces the likelihood of exhaustion after a single active day.

Sleep is another crucial factor often overlooked in the excitement of travel planning. Adjusting sleep patterns in the weeks before departure, especially if crossing time zones, can make a smoother transition upon arrival. Maintaining a consistent sleep schedule and ensuring adequate rest before the journey allows you to step off the plane feeling refreshed rather than drained.

Hydration and nutrition play a role in travel readiness as well. Drinking enough water, eating balanced meals, and ensuring sufficient vitamins and minerals in the diet contribute to overall well-being. This does not mean restrictive dieting but rather an awareness of how to fuel the body so that it feels its best when experiencing new foods, climates, and activities.

Cultivating a Travel Mindset

Beyond physical preparation, mental readiness is just as important. Traveling with an open and adaptable mindset transforms even minor inconveniences into part of the adventure. Setting intentions for the trip—whether it is to embrace spontaneity, to connect with locals, or simply to slow down and enjoy the moment—creates a personal foundation for how you wish to experience Spain.

Letting go of perfectionism is a powerful way to enhance travel enjoyment. While planning is essential, the ability to accept changes in schedule, unexpected detours, or moments of getting lost with curiosity rather than frustration makes all the difference. Viewing the trip as a fluid experience rather than a rigid checklist allows for the kind of magic that can only happen when things do not go exactly as planned.

A sense of mindfulness leading up to the trip helps as well. Whether through meditation, journaling, or simply taking quiet moments to reflect, grounding oneself in the present before the trip prevents the tendency to rush through experiences. The goal is to be fully present in Spain, to taste each bite of food, to listen to the sounds of a foreign language without distraction, to truly feel the warmth of the sun on your skin without thinking about what comes next.

Brushing Up on Essential Skills

A little preparation in practical skills goes a long way in making travel smoother. Even learning a handful of Spanish phrases before departure creates a sense of connection and confidence. Simple greetings, expressions of gratitude, and polite ways to ask for directions or order food transform interactions from transactions into meaningful exchanges.

Technology can be a helpful ally, and becoming familiar with useful travel apps ahead of time makes navigating a new country much easier. Apps for public transportation, maps that work offline, and digital language translators can all serve as helpful tools. Practicing how to use them before the trip prevents fumbling in the moment, allowing more time to enjoy the surroundings rather than staring at a phone screen in confusion.

Understanding basic cultural norms in advance also helps create positive interactions. Aware travelers take the time to learn small but significant customs, such as the later meal times in Spain, the way greetings are exchanged with cheek kisses rather than handshakes, or the fact that saying gracias after every interaction in a restaurant may actually be unnecessary. These small cultural insights demonstrate respect and enhance the feeling of being part of the place rather than just observing it.

Emotional and Personal Goals

Travel offers an opportunity for personal growth, and setting meaningful goals before departure can deepen the experience. Some travelers seek a sense of adventure, challenging themselves to try new things—perhaps tasting unfamiliar dishes, engaging in an activity that pushes comfort zones, or striking up conversations with strangers. Others view their journey as a time for reflection, a pause from daily life to gain clarity on personal goals and aspirations.

For some, the goal is simply to unwind, to disconnect from stress and allow the trip to be a full reset of mind and body. Setting boundaries before departure, such as limiting work emails or reducing social media use, ensures that the focus remains on the present experience rather than external distractions.

The anticipation leading up to a trip is as valuable as the journey itself. It is the time when excitement builds, when small preparations accumulate to create a seamless adventure, when personal goals align with the desire to fully embrace a new experience. By preparing thoughtfully, the journey to Spain becomes not just a physical trip but a deeply fulfilling experience that begins long before departure and lingers in memory long after returning home.

A vacation in Spain is a gift filled with sunshine, culture, and indulgence - an experience to be infinitely grateful for.

Building Excitement Daily

The Countdown

The moment your trip to Spain is officially on the calendar, time takes on a different quality. At first, it feels like an eternity stretches between now and the day you leave, the excitement pulsing beneath the surface but not yet urgent. Then, slowly, the weeks pass, and the countdown truly begins. With each day that draws you closer to departure, your anticipation builds. This is the time to savor the wait, to immerse yourself in preparation, and to turn the lead-up into part of the journey itself.

Three Months to Go: Laying the Groundwork

With three months until departure, the trip still feels like a distant dream, but this is the perfect time to start shaping it into reality. Now is when long-term preparations begin to take form, allowing you to enter the final stretch with ease and confidence. It is the moment to fine-tune your travel vision, ensuring that all the essential pieces fall into place without stress or last-minute scrambling.

At this stage, refining the itinerary brings a new level of excitement. Perhaps you have already decided on your main destinations, but now is the time to dive deeper. Researching neighborhoods, hidden gems, and local experiences turns abstract plans into vivid pictures. Maybe you imagine yourself wandering through the sun-drenched vineyards of La Rioja, sipping wine with the warm breeze in your hair. Or perhaps your mind drifts to a quiet Andalusian patio, where the scent of orange blossoms lingers in the air. Every detail you uncover makes the upcoming experience feel more real, adding richness to the anticipation.

This is also the perfect time to ensure all travel documents are in order. Checking the expiration date on your passport, researching visa requirements if necessary, and securing travel insurance are simple but crucial steps that eliminate unnecessary worries later. If you plan to drive in Spain, verifying whether you need an international driving permit ensures that you will not face any last-minute surprises.

For those who enjoy capturing their travels through photography, now is the time to brush up on skills or research the best locations for breathtaking shots. Understanding how to work with light, compose dynamic images, or even practice basic photography techniques means you will be able to document your journey in a way that truly captures its essence.

Two Months to Go: The Immersion Phase

With just eight weeks remaining, Spain begins to feel much closer. This is when anticipation shifts into something more tangible, and every passing day brings a sense of growing excitement. One of the best ways to enhance this period is through cultural immersion. The more you engage with Spanish culture now, the more rewarding your trip will be.

Language practice becomes particularly valuable at this stage. Even learning a few essential phrases allows for more natural interactions upon arrival. Simple greetings, polite expressions, and ordering food with confidence create a connection between traveler and local that goes beyond transactional exchanges. If speaking in full sentences feels daunting, focusing on key words and pronunciation still makes a difference. Listening to Spanish podcasts, watching Spanish films, or reading short articles in Spanish enhances familiarity with the language in a way that does not feel like studying but rather like stepping into the rhythm of Spain.

Food is another immersive gateway into the culture. Experimenting with Spanish cooking at home is both a practical and sensory way to prepare for the trip. Trying your hand at making paella, crafting the perfect tortilla de patatas, or preparing a plate of authentic jamón ibérico and manchego cheese with a glass of Spanish wine is more than just a meal. It is a way of bringing Spain into your home, allowing the flavors and aromas to transport you in anticipation of the real thing.

This is also the perfect time to finalize logistics. If train travel between cities is part of the plan, booking tickets early ensures better prices and seating options. If certain attractions require advance reservations, such as visiting the Alhambra in Granada or La Sagrada Família in Barcelona, securing those now avoids disappointment later. Even small details, like researching how public transportation works in different cities or familiarizing yourself with local customs, make the transition smoother once you arrive.

One Month to Go: The Excitement Peaks

With only four weeks remaining, the reality of the trip begins to settle in. Every conversation about it feels more thrilling, and the sense of anticipation becomes part of daily life. This is the moment when the countdown becomes something you actively engage with, not just something you wait for.

Packing lists start taking shape now, even if they are just rough drafts. Thinking about the climate, planned activities, and personal travel style helps in determining what to bring. Spain's varied geography means packing strategically. A visit to the north, where the weather is milder, requires different preparation than a trip to the sun-drenched south. Ensuring comfortable walking shoes are ready, light but stylish clothing is selected, and travel essentials are gathered makes packing a smoother process later.

This is also a great time to start visualizing the trip in a more structured way. Instead of simply imagining the trip in broad strokes, picturing specific moments enhances the excitement. Envisioning the exact café where you will have your first breakfast, the first museum or landmark you will visit, or even the feeling of stepping out onto the streets for the first time brings an added layer of anticipation.

If fitness has been part of the pre-trip preparation, now is when it begins to show results. Whether it has been increasing stamina for long walks, improving flexibility for active adventures, or simply feeling stronger and more energized, these efforts now contribute directly to making the trip more enjoyable. Travel is inherently physical, from carrying luggage through train stations to exploring on foot, and feeling prepared for these moments allows you to embrace them with enthusiasm rather than fatigue.

As the days continue to pass, small traditions can heighten the sense of countdown. Marking off days on a calendar, playing Spanish music while cooking dinner, or even setting aside time each night to read about a different aspect of Spain's history, culture, or food keeps the excitement alive. These little rituals make the anticipation part of everyday life, turning the final month into a journey of its own.

Savoring the Final Stretch

The last few weeks before a trip are an exhilarating time. Excitement blends with a touch of impatience, as the wait feels both too short and too long at once. The key is to channel this energy into meaningful preparations rather than letting the anticipation become overwhelming.

Ensuring everything is in order at home, double-checking reservations, and finalizing any last-minute details brings a sense of control and confidence. But just as importantly, allowing yourself to truly enjoy this time makes it even more special. The countdown is not just about waiting for the trip to begin. It is about making the days leading up to it as fulfilling as the journey itself.

Spain is almost within reach. Soon, you will walk its streets, hear its music, taste its food, and feel its sun on your skin. But for now, the excitement of knowing what awaits is a gift in itself. Every moment leading up to departure is another step closer to the adventure of a lifetime.

At Spanish markets,

you can immerse yourself in a colorful world,

smell aromatic spices, and discover

handcrafted treasures.

SAFE

Financial Freedom for a Perfect Trip

Enjoy carefree

A well-planned budget is the foundation of a stress-free and fulfilling vacation. Money, when thoughtfully managed, transforms from a source of concern into a gateway to experiences. Budget planning is not about restricting yourself but about creating the financial freedom to indulge in the things that truly bring joy. Knowing exactly how much you can comfortably spend enhances the excitement of the trip, allowing you to savor every meal, excursion, and unexpected opportunity without a hint of guilt.

Designing the Perfect Travel Budget

The first step to creating a solid travel budget is understanding what kind of experience you want to have. Spain offers a vast range of options, from luxurious hotels and Michelin-starred dining to charming guesthouses and budget-friendly tapas bars. Knowing what matters most to you helps in prioritizing spending. Some travelers dream of staying in a boutique hotel overlooking the Mediterranean, while others find their greatest joy in experiencing as much local cuisine as possible. Defining these priorities allows for a tailored budget that reflects your personal travel style.

Breaking down expenses into key categories ensures that nothing gets overlooked. Accommodations, transportation, food, activities, and daily spending all play a role in shaping the financial picture. Researching average costs for each category in your chosen destinations gives a realistic sense of what to expect. A stay in Madrid or Barcelona may require a higher accommodation budget than a visit to a smaller town like Salamanca or Cádiz. Dining out in San Sebastián, renowned for its culinary excellence, will likely be more expensive than enjoying a menu del día in a quiet Andalusian village.

Once you have an estimated total, planning how to save for the trip becomes the next exciting challenge. Having a clear goal transforms saving from a chore into a rewarding process. Each contribution to the travel fund becomes a step closer to sipping wine in a sunlit plaza or taking a scenic train ride through the Spanish countryside.

Turning Savings into an Enjoyable Journey

The key to successful saving is to make it feel like part of the adventure rather than a sacrifice. Viewing each saved euro as an investment in an unforgettable experience shifts the mindset from one of restriction to one of anticipation. Instead of seeing it as cutting back, it becomes an active choice to prioritize moments that will bring the most joy.

Small lifestyle adjustments can make a significant difference. Brewing coffee at home instead of buying it daily or preparing a few extra home-cooked meals each week may seem minor, but over time, these savings add up to an extra night in a beautiful Spanish hotel or a special dinner at a renowned local restaurant. Finding creative ways to save enhances the anticipation, as every small effort is a step toward something tangible and exciting.

Automating savings is a helpful strategy that takes the effort out of the process. Setting up a dedicated travel fund and directing a fixed amount toward it each month ensures steady progress without requiring constant decision-making. Watching the balance grow creates a sense of achievement, reinforcing the excitement for the trip ahead.

The Joy of Guilt-Free Spending

One of the most rewarding aspects of budget planning is the freedom it provides to spend without hesitation once the trip begins. A well-prepared budget allows you to indulge in experiences that bring genuine happiness, whether it is a flamenco show in Seville, a guided tour through the historic streets of Granada, or an exquisite multi-course meal at a seaside restaurant.

Many travelers worry about overspending on vacation, but setting realistic expectations in advance eliminates that stress. By designating specific amounts for different categories, you create a framework that allows for enjoyment without uncertainty. If the budget includes a splurge on a luxury hotel for a night or a spontaneous shopping spree in Madrid, it can be enjoyed fully, knowing it is part of the plan.

A flexible approach to budgeting ensures that there is room for unexpected delights. Sometimes, the most memorable experiences are unplanned—a charming café discovered by accident, an impromptu wine tasting at a small vineyard, or a ticket to a local festival that you did not know was happening. Leaving a portion of the budget open for spontaneous decisions enhances the sense of adventure while staying within financial comfort.

Finding Value Without Sacrificing Experience

Traveling on a budget does not mean missing out on the best experiences. In fact, some of the richest moments in Spain cost little or nothing at all. Wandering through historic quarters, admiring breathtaking architecture, lounging on pristine beaches, and exploring vibrant local markets require no admission fee yet provide immense joy.

Many of Spain's greatest culinary experiences are incredibly affordable. The tradition of free tapas in some regions, where a drink comes with a complimentary snack, allows for delicious and budget-friendly dining. Markets like La Boqueria in Barcelona or Mercado de San Miguel in Madrid offer the chance to sample fresh, high-quality food without the cost of a formal restaurant meal. In smaller towns, family-run restaurants serve generous portions of authentic Spanish dishes at prices that feel like a hidden treasure.

Transportation can also be managed wisely. Spain's extensive public transportation network offers affordable ways to explore the country. Booking train tickets in advance through RENFE often secures significant discounts, while budget-friendly bus routes connect even the most remote destinations. Walking, one of the best ways to experience Spain's cities and landscapes, is both free and deeply rewarding.

Balancing Splurges and Savings

A thoughtfully planned budget includes a balance of indulgence and practicality. Knowing where to save allows for guilt-free splurges in the areas that matter most. For some, that might mean reserving a table at one of Spain's world-famous restaurants, savoring every bite of a meticulously prepared dish. For others, it might be booking a private tour of a historical landmark, gaining exclusive insight into centuries of history. Experiences that create lasting memories are always worth the investment. A hot air balloon ride over the vineyards of La Rioja, a flamenco class in the heart of Andalusia, or a night in a luxurious parador—Spain's historic state-run hotels—may come at a higher cost, but they also offer something truly unforgettable. Budgeting for these moments in advance ensures they can be enjoyed without hesitation.

Keeping the Momentum Going

The satisfaction of a well-managed travel budget does not end when the trip is over. Reflecting on the experience and reviewing spending afterward provides valuable insight for future adventures. Identifying what brought the most joy and where adjustments could be made allows for even better financial planning on the next trip. For many travelers, budgeting for Spain is not just about one vacation. It is about creating a sustainable way to experience the world regularly. By developing smart saving habits and prioritizing travel in daily financial decisions, future trips become easier to plan and enjoy.

Every euro saved is a step toward a new adventure, and every thoughtful decision made before departure enhances the joy of the journey. When the plane lands and the first steps are taken on Spanish soil, the knowledge that everything is financially prepared creates a sense of freedom. Without stress or uncertainty, the focus remains where it should be—on the beauty, culture, and magic of Spain.

Every coin spent on vacation is an investment in unforgettable moments and cherished memories.

Savoring Spain

One Bite at a Time

To truly know Spain is to taste it. Food is not just nourishment in this country. It is tradition, identity, and an essential part of everyday life. From bustling markets filled with vibrant produce to age-old recipes passed down through generations, Spanish cuisine is a journey in itself. Each region tells its own story through flavors, aromas, and textures, inviting travelers to discover the soul of Spain one dish at a time. Whether savoring a slow-cooked paella by the Mediterranean, sampling bite-sized pintxos in a lively Basque bar, or sipping a velvety glass of Rioja in a sun-drenched vineyard, every meal is an experience to be remembered.

The Essence of Spanish Cuisine

Spanish food is defined by its simplicity, high-quality ingredients, and deep-rooted regional diversity. Unlike cuisines that rely on elaborate preparation, Spain celebrates the purity of flavors. The country's culinary landscape is shaped by its geography—fertile farmlands, rugged coastlines, and centuries-old olive groves all contribute to the richness of its dishes. Seafood thrives along the coasts, with fresh octopus, prawns, and sardines playing a central role in many traditional meals. Inland, hearty stews, aged cheeses, and cured meats reflect the agricultural heart of the country.

Olive oil is the foundation of Spanish cooking, its golden hues drizzling over salads, bread, and grilled vegetables. Garlic and onions form the backbone of many dishes, their aromas filling kitchens as they sizzle in earthenware pans. The vibrant reds of smoked paprika and saffron add depth and color, infusing dishes with a warmth that is uniquely Spanish. Meals are meant to be shared, to be enjoyed slowly, with conversation and laughter flowing as freely as the wine that accompanies them.

Regional Specialties and Timeless Traditions

Every region in Spain boasts its own culinary identity, shaped by local traditions and historical influences. In Andalusia, the birthplace of tapas, small plates of bold and flavorful bites define the dining experience. Here, one can wander from bar to bar, sampling everything from crispy fried fish to creamy **salmorejo**, a richer and thicker cousin of gazpacho, topped with finely chopped jamón and hard-boiled eggs. Catalonia offers a fusion of Mediterranean and mountain flavors. The iconic **pa amb tomàquet**—simple yet irresistible—features rustic bread rubbed with ripe tomatoes, drizzled with olive oil, and sprinkled with sea salt. In the same region, **suquet de peix**, a fragrant fish stew infused with saffron and almonds, pays homage to Catalonia's deep connection with the sea.

The Basque Country is a paradise for food lovers, where **pintxos** dominate the culinary scene. Unlike traditional tapas, pintxos are often skewered onto slices of bread, creating small, visually stunning bites bursting with flavor. From tender grilled squid to creamy **txangurro** (spider crab), these delicacies are meant to be enjoyed alongside a glass of **txakoli**, a lightly sparkling white wine that perfectly complements the region's seafood-driven cuisine. Moving inland, the mountainous landscapes of Castilla y León and La Rioja give rise to robust, meat-heavy dishes. **Cochinillo asado**, a succulent roast suckling pig, is a specialty of Segovia, its crisp golden skin yielding to melt-in-your-mouth tenderness. In contrast, **fabada asturiana**, a rich bean stew with chorizo and morcilla, warms the soul in the cooler northern regions of Asturias and Cantabria.

One cannot speak of Spanish cuisine without mentioning **paella**, the pride of Valencia. Though many variations exist, the traditional **paella valenciana** is made with rabbit, chicken, and green beans, cooked slowly in a wide, shallow pan until the rice forms a perfectly crisp layer known as **socarrat**. Seafood lovers may opt for **paella de marisco**, brimming with mussels, prawns, and calamari, kissed by the briny essence of the Mediterranean.

Sweets and Indulgences
Spain's love affair with desserts is as rich as its history. Flaky, golden **churros**, served with thick, velvety hot chocolate, are a beloved indulgence, perfect for a late-night treat or a leisurely morning in Madrid's historic cafés. In Catalonia, the delicate **crema catalana**, a cousin of France's crème brûlée, delights with its crisp caramelized top and creamy citrus-infused custard beneath.

In the south, **tarta de Santiago**, an almond-based cake dusted with powdered sugar, honors centuries-old traditions, its subtle sweetness and hint of lemon offering a taste of Spain's Moorish past. Meanwhile, the **polvorón**, a crumbly shortbread cookie, melts in the mouth with buttery richness, a staple during the holiday season but enjoyed year-round.

The Art of Spanish Drinks
A meal in Spain is never complete without the perfect drink to accompany it. The country's wine culture is legendary, producing some of the finest reds, whites, and sparkling cavas in the world. In La Rioja and Ribera del Duero, deep, full-bodied Tempranillo wines are crafted with meticulous care, their earthy undertones pairing beautifully with roasted meats and aged cheeses. In the northwestern region of Galicia, the crisp and citrusy Albariño white wine offers a refreshing counterpart to the region's exceptional seafood.

Beyond wine, Spain's drink culture extends to traditional favorites like **sangría**, a fruity, wine-based punch infused with oranges, apples, and a splash of brandy, best enjoyed on a warm afternoon. **Tinto de verano**, a simpler yet equally refreshing combination of red wine and soda, is a local favorite in the summer months. In Andalusia, **sherry** reigns supreme, its dry and nutty flavors ranging from the delicate Fino to the intensely sweet Pedro Ximénez.

For those seeking something stronger, **orxata**, a refreshing Valencian drink made from tiger nuts, offers a creamy yet dairy-free alternative. Meanwhile, Spain's love for coffee is evident in every café, where a morning **café con leche**, an afternoon **cortado**, or an after-dinner **carajillo** (coffee spiked with brandy or rum) brings comfort and ritual to the day.

Spices, Ingredients, and Cooking at Home

Spain's distinctive flavors are brought to life by its exceptional spices and ingredients. Smoked **pimentón de la Vera** lends a deep, smoky warmth to dishes, essential in seasoning everything from chorizo to stews. **Saffron**, the delicate crimson threads harvested by hand, gives paella its signature golden hue and fragrant aroma. **Sherry vinegar**, with its complex balance of acidity and sweetness, transforms even the simplest salads into something extraordinary.

Bringing a taste of Spain into your own kitchen is a wonderful way to extend the experience beyond the trip itself. Cooking Spanish dishes at home, experimenting with traditional ingredients, and sharing meals inspired by your travels keep the memories alive. Even something as simple as slicing fresh bread, drizzling it with olive oil, and pairing it with a selection of Spanish cheeses and cured meats creates an authentic moment of culinary connection.

A Journey of Taste and Tradition

To explore Spain through its cuisine is to embark on a journey of tradition, craftsmanship, and passion. Every dish tells a story, every ingredient carries history, and every meal is an invitation to slow down and savor. Whether indulging in the comforting warmth of a homemade tortilla de patatas, discovering the bold flavors of a regional specialty, or clinking glasses in a lively tapas bar, food in Spain is more than sustenance. It is a celebration of life itself.

As you prepare for your adventure, let the flavors of Spain guide your anticipation. Picture yourself in a cozy café, a steaming café con leche before you, or standing at a bustling market, inhaling the scent of ripe tomatoes and fresh seafood. Soon, these flavors will no longer be imagined. They will be yours to taste, to enjoy, and to remember long after the journey has ended.

A good paella smells of saffron, garlic, and sea breeze,

its taste blending flavorful rice, tender seafood,

and Mediterranean aromas.

Embracing the Unknown

One Moment at a Time

Every journey is an open invitation to the unexpected. No matter how much planning is done, no matter how many guidebooks are read or maps are studied, travel has a way of surprising even the most prepared adventurer. The true magic of any trip lies not just in the destinations but in the experiences that unfold along the way—the people met, the cultures encountered, and the moments that could never have been anticipated. Spain, with its warmth, history, and passion for life, offers an endless array of new experiences waiting to be embraced.

The Thrill of Meeting New People

One of the greatest joys of travel is the connections made along the way. Whether it is a fleeting conversation with a local shopkeeper, a shared meal with fellow travelers, or a deep discussion with someone whose perspective challenges your own, these encounters shape the experience in ways that no monument or museum ever could. Spaniards, known for their hospitality and love of conversation, welcome visitors with an openness that makes every interaction feel like an opportunity for discovery.

Walking into a neighborhood bar in Madrid, you might find yourself chatting with an elderly couple who have been coming to the same café for decades, their stories weaving a picture of the city's transformation over time. In a small Andalusian village, a local farmer might proudly explain the process of making olive oil, his passion for his craft as rich as the golden liquid itself. In Barcelona, an artist selling handmade ceramics may tell you about the inspiration behind her designs, giving new meaning to the piece you choose to take home.

Even among fellow travelers, the shared experience of exploring Spain creates instant connections. A conversation struck up while watching the sunset over the Alhambra could lead to an evening of shared tapas and laughter. A chance meeting on a hiking trail in the Picos de Europa may introduce you to a like-minded adventurer whose journey intertwines with yours for a few days. These encounters remind us that the world is filled with stories waiting to be heard, and sometimes the most memorable part of a trip is not the places seen but the people met along the way.

The Joy of Discovering New Places

No two places in Spain are the same. Each city, each village, each stretch of coastline offers something unique, a different rhythm of life waiting to be experienced. The beauty of exploring new places is in the contrast—the way a bustling metropolis like Madrid hums with energy while a quiet town in the Spanish countryside moves to a slower, more deliberate beat.

Stepping into a new city for the first time is a moment unlike any other. The streets are unfamiliar, the sounds and smells foreign yet enticing. The first few hours in a new destination are spent absorbing everything—the way the light reflects off historic buildings, the scent of freshly baked bread drifting from a nearby panadería, the way locals navigate their daily routines. With each step, the city begins to reveal itself, unfolding like a story that is yours to interpret.

Beyond the cities, Spain's landscapes provide endless opportunities for exploration. The rugged coastline of the Costa Brava, where hidden coves and turquoise waters offer secluded escapes, feels worlds apart from the rolling vineyards of La Rioja, where the land itself seems to breathe with history. The Moorish architecture of Granada stands in stark contrast to the Celtic heritage of Galicia, where misty forests and ancient ruins whisper of legends long past. Each place offers its own perspective on Spain, reminding travelers that no single journey can capture its full essence.

Experiencing Culture in Its Purest Form

Culture is not just something that exists in museums or historical sites. It lives in the rhythm of daily life, in the traditions passed down through generations, in the way people gather, celebrate, and express themselves. Experiencing a new culture is more than just witnessing it. It is about stepping into it, engaging with it, allowing it to shift your perspective.

Music is one of the most powerful ways to connect with a culture, and in Spain, it is everywhere. A walk through the streets of Seville might lead to the sound of a flamenco guitarist, his fingers dancing over the strings with an intensity that speaks of centuries-old traditions. In the Basque Country, a street festival could introduce you to the rhythmic sounds of txalaparta, an ancient percussion instrument played with wooden sticks, its beats echoing the heartbeat of the region. In a small coastal town, a group of locals might break into spontaneous song over a shared meal, their voices blending in a harmony that needs no explanation.

Festivals provide another glimpse into Spain's cultural heartbeat. The fire and passion of Las Fallas in Valencia, where giant sculptures are set ablaze in a dramatic spectacle, contrasts with the solemn beauty of Semana Santa processions, where hooded figures march through the streets carrying centuries of religious devotion on their shoulders. In the tomato-stained streets of Buñol, La Tomatina turns an entire town into a playground of pure joy, proving that sometimes, culture is best experienced not through observation but through participation.

Food, too, is a gateway to culture. Sitting down for a late-night dinner in Spain, where meals stretch for hours and conversation flows effortlessly, is to understand that here, food is about more than sustenance. It is about connection, tradition, and pleasure. Watching a jamón ibérico carver meticulously slice paper-thin pieces of cured ham or witnessing the careful layering of a traditional Spanish tortilla reminds you that behind every dish is a story, a craft perfected over time.

Stepping Outside Comfort Zones

The most transformative travel experiences often come from stepping outside the familiar. It is in the moments of uncertainty, when ordering food in a language not fully mastered, navigating unfamiliar streets, or trying an activity that feels entirely new, that growth happens. Spain provides countless opportunities to embrace the unknown.

For some, this might mean joining a local dance class in Madrid, moving to the rhythm of flamenco with no concern for perfection but only for feeling the music. For others, it could be embarking on the Camino de Santiago, walking for days through Spain's countryside, finding clarity in the simplicity of putting one foot in front of the other. It might be tasting something completely foreign—a bite of octopus in Galicia, a spoonful of rabbit paella in Valencia, or a sip of vermouth in a small neighborhood bar. Each time comfort is traded for curiosity, the reward is a deeper, richer experience. The nervous excitement of trying something new eventually fades, replaced by a sense of accomplishment, a newfound confidence, and a memory that lingers long after the trip ends.

The Lasting Impact of New Experiences

No trip leaves a traveler unchanged. The experiences collected along the way shape perspectives, broaden understanding, and create stories that become part of who we are. Long after leaving Spain, the memories remain—the scent of orange blossoms in Seville, the sound of waves crashing against the cliffs of Asturias, the taste of that first bite of churro dipped into thick, rich chocolate.

More than just moments, these experiences become part of a personal narrative, influencing how the world is seen and understood. They remind us that the greatest joys often come from the unexpected, that every encounter has the potential to teach, and that every journey is a chance to discover not just new places, but new versions of ourselves.

With each trip, a traveler collects not just souvenirs, but pieces of the world that stay with them forever. And as Spain leaves its imprint, the excitement for future adventures only grows, knowing that there are always more people to meet, more places to explore, and more moments to experience that cannot yet be imagined.

In Spain, there is something new to discover around every corner - vibrant markets, hidden alleys, and unforgettable experiences are waiting for you!

Keeping Spain Alive in Everyday Life

Vacation vibes at home

The magic of a journey does not have to end when the plane lands and daily life resumes. A vacation is not just a series of days spent in a different place. It is a state of mind, a collection of moments, emotions, and discoveries that can continue to bring joy long after returning home. Spain, with its vibrant energy, rich culture, and deep appreciation for beauty, offers countless ways to weave the spirit of travel into everyday life. By bringing elements of the trip into your home, your routines, and even your mindset, the feeling of being in Spain lingers, transforming ordinary days into a continuation of the adventure.

A Home Filled with Memories

The places visited, the meals enjoyed, and the atmosphere experienced all contribute to the unique energy of a trip. Replicating even a small part of that feeling at home turns a house into a personal travel diary, filled with reminders of beautiful moments. Souvenirs, if chosen thoughtfully, become more than objects. They carry the essence of the journey, evoking the scents, sounds, and sensations of Spain with a single glance. A hand-painted ceramic bowl from Andalusia, a delicate lace fan from Seville, or a bottle of olive oil from a sun-drenched grove in Jaén brings back the warmth of Spanish afternoons with every use.

The way a space is decorated influences mood and memory. Introducing Spanish colors and textures into a home creates an environment that feels both inviting and inspiring. Warm terracotta, deep cobalt blue, and sunlit yellows echo the streets of southern Spain, where Moorish architecture and Mediterranean influence blend in perfect harmony. Wrought iron details, rustic wooden furniture, or even a simple table set with Spanish pottery adds a touch of Iberian charm. Hanging a framed print of a favorite Spanish city or a black-and-white photograph of a bustling tapas bar instantly transports the mind back to those unforgettable places.

Scent is another powerful trigger of memories. A well-placed candle with the aroma of orange blossoms recreates the feeling of wandering through Seville's courtyards. A few sprigs of dried lavender recall the rolling countryside of Castilla-La Mancha. The rich, earthy smell of ground coffee brewing in the morning mirrors the way each Spanish day begins. These small details, seemingly insignificant on their own, combine to create an atmosphere that keeps Spain close to the heart.

A Taste of Spain in the Kitchen

One of the most satisfying ways to relive a trip is through food. The flavors that define a journey remain etched in memory, and recreating them at home brings a piece of that experience back to life. Cooking Spanish dishes does not require mastery, only enthusiasm and a willingness to experiment. The simplest meals are often the most authentic, and many of Spain's most beloved dishes rely on a few high-quality ingredients.

Breakfast can transport you instantly to a café in Madrid with nothing more than a plate of **pan con tomate**, crusty bread rubbed with fresh tomatoes, drizzled with olive oil, and sprinkled with salt. A light dinner of **tortilla española**, the classic Spanish omelet made with eggs, potatoes, and onions, fills a home with the unmistakable scent of a traditional Spanish kitchen. Tapas nights recreate the social aspect of Spanish dining, with small plates of **patatas bravas**, **gambas al ajillo**, and **jamón ibérico** shared among family or friends.

Drinks bring their own magic. Pouring a glass of **Rioja** wine or mixing a homemade **tinto de verano** instantly recalls the warmth of Spanish evenings. A pitcher of **sangría**, with slices of oranges and apples floating lazily in a deep red wine blend, turns an ordinary summer afternoon into a celebration. Even a simple espresso, served in a small cup with a square of dark chocolate, echoes the leisurely pace of Spain's café culture.

Hosting a Spanish-themed dinner transports guests straight to the Iberian Peninsula. A long, slow meal, served in multiple courses with no rush to finish, mirrors the Spanish appreciation for food as an experience rather than a necessity. Soft Spanish guitar music playing in the background, candles flickering like the glow of a tapas bar, and a toast to good company complete the illusion. The joy of travel is in sharing, and inviting others to experience the flavors of Spain keeps its spirit alive.

Bringing Spain into Everyday Life

Beyond food and décor, Spain's approach to life offers valuable lessons in finding joy in the present moment. The Spanish way of embracing leisure, prioritizing connection, and celebrating life's small pleasures can be adopted anywhere, regardless of location.

The tradition of **la sobremesa**, the unhurried time spent at the table after a meal, is one of Spain's most cherished customs. It is a reminder that meals are not meant to be rushed, that conversation and laughter are just as important as the food itself. Even if only once a week, allowing extra time to simply sit, talk, and enjoy the company of others keeps this tradition alive.

A midday pause, inspired by the Spanish siesta, does not have to mean sleep. It can be a moment to step away from the day's demands, to sit in the sun with a book, or to close the eyes and let the mind wander. Spain's slower pace is not a sign of laziness but a recognition that life is meant to be savored. Carrying this mindset home creates space for relaxation in a world that often demands constant movement.

Evenings can take inspiration from Spanish nightlife, where the streets remain alive with conversation long after sunset. A simple walk after dinner, enjoying the cool night air and the sound of distant laughter, brings a touch of Spain's energy into the night. Weekends, instead of being filled with errands, can become an opportunity to explore new neighborhoods, visit farmers' markets, or simply sit at a café watching the world go by.

Music, Film, and Literature as a Portal to Spain

One of the easiest ways to keep the Spanish spirit alive is through music. A playlist of **flamenco guitar**, **Spanish pop**, or **traditional folk songs** instantly transports the listener to a plaza in Seville or a beachside bar in Ibiza. The rhythms of **Paco de Lucía**, **Rosalía**, or **Buika** carry the soul of Spain across any distance.

Spanish cinema provides another window into the culture, offering glimpses of its landscapes, humor, and storytelling traditions. Films like **"Volver"**, **"Pan's Labyrinth"**, or **"The Secret in Their Eyes"** capture the depth and emotion of Spanish storytelling, while documentaries on Spanish cuisine, wine, or history deepen the connection to the country's heritage.

Reading also extends the journey. A novel set in Spain, whether it is a classic like **"The Shadow of the Wind"** by Carlos Ruiz Zafón or a travel memoir recounting life in an Andalusian village, allows the imagination to continue wandering. Even poetry, like the works of **Federico García Lorca**, carries the essence of Spain in its verses.

Keeping the Travel Spirit Alive

The feeling of being on vacation is not about escaping daily life. It is about engaging with the world with curiosity, openness, and appreciation. Spain teaches travelers how to embrace beauty, flavor, and spontaneity, lessons that do not need to be left behind. By bringing pieces of the trip into daily routines, whether through music, food, traditions, or mindset, the journey never truly ends.

Travel changes people. It leaves traces in the way they think, in the way they see the world, in the way they find joy in the simplest moments. Spain, with its warmth and passion, offers more than just memories. It offers a way of living that, once experienced, stays forever. Even when miles away, the heart can always return to Spain, again and again, with just a sip of wine, a familiar song, or a sunset that reminds you of the one you once watched from a Spanish terrace, lost in the beauty of the moment.

Spanish olive oil is rich in antioxidants and unsaturated fats,

proven to protect the heart, reduce inflammation,

and give the skin a radiant glow

- a true liquid gold for health and enjoyment!

Shaping Your Dream Vacation

Expectations for the vacation

Every trip is an opportunity to step away from the ordinary and embrace something new. The journey to Spain is not just about seeing famous landmarks or tasting delicious food. It is about the feelings the trip evokes, the moments that linger long after returning home, and the choices made along the way that shape the experience. A vacation is a personal canvas, and the way it unfolds depends on the expectations, mindset, and intentions set before departure. By striking a balance between planning and spontaneity, between exploration and relaxation, and between excitement and tranquility, a trip becomes more than just a break from routine. It becomes a deeply fulfilling experience.

Setting Meaningful Intentions for the Journey

Before setting foot in Spain, it helps to reflect on what this trip truly means. Every traveler has different hopes for their time away. Some seek adventure, eager to explore hidden alleys, climb scenic viewpoints, and dive headfirst into unfamiliar surroundings. Others long for rest, for slow mornings with coffee in a sunlit square, for afternoons spent by the sea, for evenings filled with nothing but the gentle hum of a distant guitar. Some are drawn to history, imagining themselves stepping back in time as they walk through ancient cities, while others want to immerse themselves in the culture, learning a few Spanish phrases, chatting with locals, and savoring the rhythm of daily life.

Being clear about personal expectations helps ensure that the trip aligns with what is most meaningful. If the goal is to reconnect with family, then the focus might be on creating shared experiences—enjoying long meals together, playing on the beach, or simply being present in each other's company without distraction. If the trip is about personal growth, it could mean stepping out of the comfort zone, trying something new, or embracing the uncertainty of travel with an open mind. There is no right or wrong way to experience Spain. The most important thing is to be honest about what will bring the greatest sense of joy and fulfillment.

Finding the Balance Between Planning and Spontaneity

While it is natural to have a list of places to see and things to do, allowing room for spontaneity often leads to the most cherished experiences. Some of the best moments in travel happen when plans shift, when an unexpected street performance captivates attention, when a small café tucked away from the crowds offers the best meal of the trip, or when a conversation with a local leads to an unplanned adventure. A flexible approach ensures that no day feels like an obligation. Instead of filling every hour with scheduled activities, leaving space for wandering and discovery allows the city or landscape to unfold naturally. The joy of walking through a new place without a specific agenda, following curiosity rather than an itinerary, brings a sense of freedom that structured plans sometimes limit. It is in these moments that true connection with a destination happens—not just through what is seen, but through what is felt. Even in well-planned activities, it is important to allow for change. Maybe the desire to see every major attraction fades in favor of a leisurely afternoon people-watching in a plaza. Maybe an unexpected craving leads to a restaurant not on the list, and it turns out to be the most memorable meal of the trip. By letting go of the idea that everything must be checked off, the experience remains fluid and enjoyable rather than feeling like a task to complete.

Embracing the Joy of Presence

In daily life, distractions are constant. Work, responsibilities, and digital noise often pull attention away from the present moment. A vacation is an opportunity to break free from this pattern, to truly be where you are, to absorb the surroundings fully without thinking ahead to the next thing. Consciously deciding to be present—to engage all the senses, to notice small details, to listen deeply—transforms an ordinary day into something extraordinary.

There is something powerful about watching the sunset over the rooftops of Seville, not through the lens of a camera but with eyes that truly take in the shifting colors of the sky. The simple act of sipping a glass of wine, feeling its warmth spread through the body, becomes an experience in itself. Tasting food slowly, savoring every bite, rather than rushing through a meal, allows for appreciation of the craftsmanship behind it. Walking through a historic district, running fingers along centuries-old stone walls, imagining the people who walked there before, brings history to life in a way no textbook ever could.

This kind of presence extends to the people around you. If traveling with family or friends, making a conscious effort to be in the moment strengthens connections. Setting aside phones during meals, engaging in deep conversations, and sharing laughter over inside jokes or unexpected mishaps create memories that last far beyond the trip itself. Travel has a way of bringing people closer, but only if there is space for true connection.

Letting Go of Pressure and Expectations

One of the quickest ways to diminish the joy of a vacation is to place unnecessary pressure on it. High expectations—whether about how the trip should feel, how much should be accomplished, or how perfect every moment should be—can lead to disappointment. Instead of aiming for an idealized version of the trip, embracing it as it unfolds allows for a much richer experience.

Not every day will go as planned. There may be moments of fatigue, of getting lost, of dealing with unexpected challenges. A wrong turn might lead to a hidden gem of a neighborhood. A delayed plan might result in a spontaneous and more fulfilling alternative. The mindset brought into these situations determines whether they are seen as frustrations or as part of the adventure.

Travel does not have to be perfect to be meaningful. The best experiences often come from the things that do not go as expected. Laughter at a mispronounced Spanish phrase, the discovery of an unknown dish that becomes a new favorite, or even a rainy afternoon spent in a cozy café instead of at a planned outdoor excursion—all of these create the richness of the journey.

Allowing Time for Reflection

A vacation is not just about collecting experiences. It is also about understanding what those experiences mean. Taking time during the trip to reflect—whether through journaling, quiet moments alone, or conversations with travel companions—enhances the depth of the experience. What has stood out the most? What feelings have surfaced? What unexpected lessons has Spain taught?

Journaling, even if just a few sentences a day, captures small details that might otherwise fade over time. The way the air smelled in a certain square, the laughter of children playing soccer in the streets, the sensation of stepping into the cool waters of the Mediterranean—these small moments often hold the most meaning. Looking back on these reflections later allows the experience to remain alive long after returning home.

Even simple mental check-ins throughout the day bring awareness to the experience. Pausing to take a deep breath, to feel gratitude for being in this place at this time, to acknowledge the privilege of travel—these small acts create a deeper sense of fulfillment. The goal is not just to go somewhere new but to return feeling enriched, with a fresh perspective and a heart full of memories.

Carrying the Vacation Spirit Forward

The best trips do not truly end. They continue in the way they shift perspectives, in the habits brought home, in the appreciation gained for different ways of living. Whether it is adopting Spain's slower pace, making time for long meals, or embracing a more spontaneous approach to daily life, the lessons learned on the journey can continue far beyond the trip itself.

Expectations shape experiences, but the most rewarding moments often come when expectations are set aside in favor of discovery. A vacation is not about perfection. It is about presence. It is about embracing the unknown with excitement rather than fear. It is about making choices that align with what brings the greatest joy. And above all, it is about remembering that travel is not just about seeing new places. It is about experiencing them with an open heart, a curious mind, and a spirit ready to embrace whatever comes next.

Relaxation begins the moment you travel to Spain, as anticipation builds for sunny beaches, Mediterranean joie de vivre, and the first delicious tapas.

Savoring the Final Countdown

The vacation is about to begin

The last week before departure carries a special kind of energy. Excitement builds with every passing day, the anticipation almost tangible. Soon, the ordinary routines of daily life will be replaced by sun-drenched streets, the sound of Spanish conversations flowing around you, and the thrill of stepping into a new adventure. This final stretch is not just about checking off tasks. It is about easing into the vacation mindset, allowing the transition from the familiar to the extraordinary to feel seamless and joyful. By managing responsibilities, embracing the pre-travel excitement, and making space to enjoy the wait, the journey begins long before the plane takes off.

The Art of a Smooth Departure

A trip feels most enjoyable when there are no loose ends left behind. The last thing anyone wants is to be sitting at a café in Madrid, sipping a rich café con leche, only to have thoughts of unfinished work creeping in. The final workdays before departure should be approached with intention, ensuring that all responsibilities are handled before stepping away. It helps to create a clear plan for wrapping up projects, notifying colleagues, and setting up automated responses for emails. Letting people know in advance that you will be unavailable during your travels reduces the chances of last-minute demands, allowing for a more peaceful departure.

Equally important is making sure that everything at home is in order. Knowing that bills are paid, pets are cared for, and plants will be watered brings a sense of ease. Arranging for a neighbor or family member to check on things adds an extra layer of reassurance. Even small details, like setting up light timers or leaving a clean home to return to, create a smooth transition back when the trip eventually comes to an end.

Packing should not be a rushed, stressful task squeezed into the final night. Instead, spreading it out over the week allows for a more thoughtful approach. Starting with a list ensures that nothing essential is forgotten, from travel documents to comfortable walking shoes. Packing gradually also brings a sense of excitement, each added item serving as a reminder of the adventure ahead. Holding a freshly folded summer dress, a pair of sunglasses, or a lightweight travel book in your hands makes the trip feel all the more real.

Bringing the Vacation Energy into Daily Life

A common mistake in the final week before a trip is to remain entirely focused on logistics, forgetting to enjoy the excitement of what is coming. The transition into vacation mode does not have to wait until arrival in Spain. It can begin right now, by infusing everyday life with elements of the journey ahead. One of the best ways to do this is through food. Visiting a Spanish restaurant, ordering a plate of patatas bravas, dipping fresh bread into golden olive oil, and sipping a glass of Rioja is a sensory way to bring the destination closer. If dining out is not an option, preparing a simple Spanish meal at home—perhaps a tortilla de patatas or a chilled gazpacho—allows the flavors of Spain to set the tone for the upcoming adventure.

Music has the power to shift moods instantly, making it another perfect way to cultivate the vacation spirit. Creating a playlist filled with Spanish guitar, flamenco rhythms, or even contemporary Spanish pop artists builds excitement. Playing it during morning coffee, in the car, or while cooking strengthens the connection to the trip, turning daily moments into pre-travel celebrations.

Watching Spanish films or travel documentaries also helps bring the destination to life before arrival. A beautifully shot film set in Spain immerses the mind in the country's landscapes and atmosphere. A travel documentary showcasing hidden villages or traditional festivals sparks inspiration for last-minute itinerary ideas. Even flipping through a photo book of Spain, filled with vibrant market scenes and sunlit coastlines, ignites a sense of wonder.

Embracing the Final Days with Intention

Rather than rushing through the last week in a flurry of preparation, treating it as an essential part of the journey makes the experience richer. Taking time to appreciate the anticipation, to let the excitement build, turns the wait into something to be enjoyed rather than endured. One way to do this is through mindful reflection. Sitting down with a journal and writing about what excites you most about the trip, what you hope to experience, and how you want to feel while there brings a deeper awareness to the journey ahead. This also helps in setting personal intentions—whether it is to travel with a sense of openness, to embrace spontaneity, or to fully immerse in the culture.

Spending quality time with loved ones before departure adds another layer of joy to the final week. If traveling with family or friends, setting aside an evening to talk about what everyone is looking forward to enhances the shared excitement. If traveling alone, meeting up with close friends for a farewell dinner or a relaxed afternoon walk ensures that the time before departure is filled with meaningful moments rather than just tasks.

Making space for rest is just as important as preparing. Ensuring that the last few nights include good sleep prevents exhaustion from setting in before the trip even begins. A well-rested traveler arrives in Spain ready to embrace every experience, rather than feeling drained from last-minute stress. Creating a relaxing evening routine—perhaps with a cup of herbal tea, soft lighting, and a book about Spain—helps signal to the body and mind that a period of adventure and renewal is about to begin.

The Night Before Departure

The final night before a trip carries a unique kind of excitement. The suitcase stands ready, the passport is tucked into place, and the reality of leaving has fully settled in. This is not the time to be scrambling for missing items or staying up late trying to finish last-minute preparations. Instead, it should be a moment of quiet anticipation, of soaking in the realization that the journey is finally here.

Taking a final walk through the house, making sure everything is set, and setting out a comfortable travel outfit for the next day brings a sense of ease. A warm shower, a light meal, and a brief moment of stillness—perhaps sitting with a cup of tea or looking at photos of Spain one last time before sleep—create a peaceful transition into the journey ahead.

Lying in bed, with the suitcase packed and the alarm set, the mind begins to wander. Thoughts drift to the moment of arrival, to the first breath of Spanish air, to the feeling of stepping into a sunlit square and hearing the hum of life in a new place. Excitement tingles in the chest, making it difficult to sleep, yet there is comfort in knowing that tomorrow, the adventure begins.

The final week before departure is not just a countdown. It is an essential part of the journey, a time to prepare, to celebrate, and to fully embrace the anticipation. By stepping into vacation mode early, by wrapping up responsibilities with ease, and by savoring the excitement rather than rushing through it, the transition into travel becomes effortless. The beauty of a trip is not just in the destination but in the way it unfolds, from the very first spark of excitement to the final moments before stepping onto the plane. And now, the wait is almost over. Spain is calling, and soon, the adventure will no longer be imagined. It will be real.

Every year, over 80 million people travel to Spain to experience its beauty and diversity - and you are one of the lucky ones!

The Art of Packing

A Ritual of Anticipation

Packing is more than just filling a suitcase. It is the transition between everyday life and adventure, the moment when the trip stops being an idea and becomes something tangible. Every carefully chosen item carries the promise of experiences to come, each folded shirt and neatly placed pair of shoes marking the beginning of a journey. The process itself is a ritual, a way of mentally and emotionally preparing for the change ahead. The weight of the suitcase in hand signals that the wait is over. The adventure is no longer distant. It is about to begin.

The Joy of Packing

There is something undeniably exciting about laying out everything that will accompany a journey. With each item selected, a vision of the trip begins to take shape. The lightweight linen shirt is not just clothing. It is the feeling of strolling through sunlit Spanish plazas. The comfortable sandals are more than footwear. They represent the long walks through historic streets, the slow meandering along the beach, the moments of pausing to take in a breathtaking view. The travel journal, the sunglasses, the perfectly chosen novel for the flight—each piece carries an intention, a small part of the story that will unfold.

Packing forces a moment of reflection, a chance to consider what is truly needed and what can be left behind. It is an exercise in simplicity, in curating the essentials that will support rather than burden the experience. Unlike everyday life, where possessions accumulate, travel demands selectiveness. A suitcase is a microcosm of what is most important, a carefully chosen collection of what will enhance the days ahead.

The process also brings anticipation into focus. Folding clothes, zipping compartments, and making final selections serve as a reminder that soon, these belongings will no longer be resting in a familiar space. They will be in Spain, part of a new landscape, a different rhythm of life. The journey is no longer a distant plan. It is happening.

The Art of Packing Light

There is an elegance to packing light, a freedom that comes with carrying only what is necessary. The less weighed down a traveler is, the more room there is for spontaneity, for ease of movement, for a sense of unburdened exploration. Overpacking often stems from the fear of not having enough, but in reality, most trips require far less than expected. A well-packed suitcase is one that holds only what will truly be used, with each item earning its place through versatility and necessity.

Choosing a color scheme simplifies packing, allowing for mix-and-match outfits that require fewer individual pieces. Lightweight, breathable fabrics make travel more comfortable, especially in Spain's warm climate. Shoes, often the most cumbersome items, should be carefully selected—one pair for walking, one for casual outings, and perhaps one for a more formal evening. Accessories like scarves or jewelry add variety without adding bulk, transforming outfits with minimal effort.

Beyond clothing, travel essentials should be chosen with thoughtfulness. A high-quality travel adapter ensures that devices remain charged. A compact, refillable water bottle is invaluable, especially in Spain's warm regions. A small pack of essentials for the plane—lip balm, hand lotion, and a sleep mask—makes long flights more comfortable. Travel documents, insurance details, and a copy of important reservations should be easily accessible, providing peace of mind.

Packing as a Mental Shift

The moment a suitcase is zipped shut, a shift occurs. The mind moves from the routines of home to the freedom of travel. The trip feels closer, more immediate. The excitement becomes less abstract and more real. This transition is an essential part of the journey, a way of stepping out of daily life and into a new mindset.

There is a beauty in knowing that everything needed is contained within a single bag. It is a reminder that experiences matter more than possessions, that adventure thrives in simplicity. Traveling light creates a sense of clarity, a focus on what is truly important. The less packed, the more space there is to collect memories, to bring back souvenirs that hold meaning rather than just things.

Packing is also a way of setting intentions for the trip. The act of choosing what to bring mirrors the choices made during travel. Will this trip be one of long city walks, of early mornings exploring markets, of late nights enjoying music in a lively square? Or will it be one of relaxation, of slow afternoons by the sea, of quiet moments with a book and a view? The contents of a suitcase tell the story before it is even lived.

The Final Checklist

Before the suitcase is closed for the last time, a final checklist ensures that nothing important is forgotten. Essentials come first: passport, tickets, travel insurance, and any necessary documents for accommodations or transportation. A small amount of local currency is useful for arrival, making it easy to pay for a taxi, a coffee, or a first meal without searching for an ATM.

Technology must also be accounted for. A phone charger, power bank, and any necessary adapters prevent the frustration of dead batteries in unfamiliar places. A camera or smartphone with enough storage space ensures that moments can be captured without hesitation. Noise-canceling headphones make flights more comfortable, while an e-reader or a well-chosen book provides company during quiet moments.

Toiletries should be packed with efficiency in mind. Travel-sized containers save space, and a small first aid kit with essentials like pain relievers, motion sickness tablets, and bandages prepares for minor inconveniences. Sunscreen and lip balm with SPF protect against the strong Spanish sun. A lightweight tote bag or backpack is invaluable for daily outings, holding everything needed while exploring.

Comfort is key during travel, so a carefully chosen outfit for the journey matters. Layers work best, allowing for adjustments to changing temperatures. A soft scarf or shawl doubles as a blanket during flights. Slip-on shoes make security checks easier. The goal is to step onto the plane feeling relaxed, comfortable, and ready for what comes next.

The Moment of Departure

With the suitcase packed, the anticipation reaches its peak. The house is left behind, the airport comes into view, and the adventure officially begins. There is a certain joy in wheeling a suitcase through a terminal, in hearing the final boarding call, in settling into a seat knowing that the next stop is Spain. The world shifts in these moments. Everything familiar is paused, and something new begins.

Packing is not just about preparation. It is about embracing the excitement, the transformation, the shift from the known to the unknown. It is the last step before departure and the first step into adventure. The moment the suitcase closes, the trip is no longer just an idea. It is real. It is happening. And soon, every item carefully packed will find its place in a new story, one that is waiting to be written.

Opening your suitcase releases the scent of past journeys - a hint of sunscreen and sea breeze. But with every freshly packed piece of clothing, it transforms into the promising freshness of a new adventure.

Travel with Ease

Embracing the Unexpected

No matter how carefully a trip is planned, the unexpected will always find a way to appear. A delayed flight, a sudden change in weather, a missed connection, or an unexpected detour can shift the course of events in ways that no itinerary could predict. But the beauty of travel lies not in its predictability but in its spontaneity. The most memorable experiences often come from the unplanned, from the moments that force travelers to adapt, to laugh at the absurd, and to let go of the illusion of control. Serenity is the secret to turning disruptions into opportunities, to transforming what seems like an inconvenience into a new adventure.

The Inevitability of the Unexpected

Every journey carries an element of unpredictability. Even the most meticulous traveler, armed with confirmations, reservations, and backup plans, will eventually encounter something that veers from expectation. It could be something small, like a restaurant being closed upon arrival, or something significant, like a missed train connection that requires a complete change of plans. The key is not to fear these moments but to welcome them as part of the journey.

When stepping into a new environment, unfamiliar rules and customs shape the experience in ways that cannot always be anticipated. A museum may be unexpectedly closed for a holiday, a public transportation strike might change the day's itinerary, or a hotel reservation may have been misplaced in the system. These moments test patience, but they also present an opportunity to slow down and embrace an alternative path.

Sometimes, a missed opportunity leads to a different but equally rewarding experience. The restaurant that was closed may lead to the discovery of a hidden family-owned café with the best tortilla española in town. The unexpected delay in a train station might result in a conversation with a fellow traveler, exchanging stories and laughter while waiting for the next departure.

Staying Calm and Composed

The ability to remain calm in the face of the unexpected is a skill that transforms a trip from stressful to enjoyable. When disruptions occur, taking a deep breath and assessing the situation with a clear mind prevents frustration from taking over. Instead of reacting with panic, pausing for a moment allows for rational thinking and creative problem-solving.

Perspective is everything. What feels like a major problem in the moment is often just a minor inconvenience in the grand scheme of the trip. If a flight is delayed, it is an opportunity to relax at the airport café with a book. If a planned excursion gets canceled, the newfound free time can be used for spontaneous exploration. Shifting the focus from what is going wrong to what is still possible makes all the difference.

Keeping a sense of humor also lightens the weight of unexpected mishaps. Travel is full of moments that do not go according to plan, but those are often the stories that are retold with laughter long after the trip has ended. Getting lost in a new city, struggling with language barriers, or ordering something entirely different than expected at a restaurant can become cherished memories rather than frustrations.

A Plan for Handling the Unexpected

While the unexpected cannot be controlled, having a flexible mindset and a few simple strategies can make navigating challenges easier. Preparation helps, but adaptability is the real key. Being prepared means having access to important travel information, like knowing alternative transportation routes, carrying backup copies of important documents, and having a small emergency fund set aside for unforeseen expenses. But beyond preparation, the ability to shift plans with ease is what makes the biggest difference.

One of the most useful tools is an attitude of curiosity rather than resistance. When something does not go as planned, asking, "What else can I do with this moment?" rather than "Why is this happening?" shifts frustration into exploration. A canceled event may open the door to discovering a charming neighborhood that was not originally on the itinerary. A wrong turn down an unfamiliar street could lead to an unforgettable sunset view. Technology can also be a great ally in navigating the unexpected. Travel apps help find alternative routes, translation tools assist in communication, and digital maps make it easier to reorient when lost. But just as important as technology is the willingness to ask for help. Locals often have the best solutions, and a simple question to a passerby can lead to insider tips that no guidebook could provide.

The Importance of Serenity

Serenity is the foundation of a relaxed and fulfilling journey. It allows travelers to experience each moment as it comes, without clinging to expectations or fearing change. A calm mind makes better decisions, finds joy in the little things, and embraces the imperfections that make travel so unique.

Finding moments of stillness, even in the busiest parts of a trip, helps cultivate this sense of peace. Sitting quietly in a plaza, watching the world go by, or taking a slow walk along the coastline without rushing to the next destination keeps the mind grounded. Accepting that not everything needs to be controlled or planned makes space for spontaneity, and it is often in those unplanned moments that the most beautiful parts of a trip unfold.
Letting go of the pressure to have a "perfect" trip is also essential. There is no such thing as a flawless travel experience, and the pursuit of perfection often leads to unnecessary stress. The goal should not be to fit everything into a rigid plan but to fully experience the moments that do happen, whether they were expected or not.

Turning the Unexpected into a Gift

Some of the best travel experiences happen by accident. A conversation with a stranger leads to an invitation to a local celebration. A wrong turn reveals a hidden viewpoint that no tourist guide mentions. A missed bus results in a peaceful hour spent wandering through a park, discovering its beauty without intention. These are the moments that make travel feel magical, reminding travelers that sometimes, the best experiences are the ones that were never planned at all.

By shifting the mindset from frustration to curiosity, from resistance to acceptance, every twist in the journey becomes an opportunity rather than an obstacle. Travel is not about controlling every detail. It is about being open to what unfolds, about embracing both the expected and the unexpected with the same sense of wonder.

The beauty of Spain, and of travel itself, is not just in the landmarks, the food, or the carefully planned itineraries. It is in the way each day brings something new, in the moments of surprise that add depth to the experience. The unexpected is not an interruption of the journey. It is the journey itself. And when approached with serenity, every moment—whether planned or not—becomes part of a story worth telling.

Trips to Spain write their own stories - filled with unforgettable moments that resonate long after they end.

The Magic of Returning Travelers

Motivation Through a Change of Perspective

At the airport, train station, or a highway rest stop—places where travelers from around the world converge—the end of one journey often meets the beginning of another. While you wait eagerly to embark on your adventure, others are returning home, walking past you with the weary yet fulfilled expressions of those who have just completed a journey of their own. In their faces and gestures, you can see exhaustion but also the quiet joy of cherished moments. This fleeting encounter, where your departure meets their return, is rich with meaning. The returning travelers invite you to reflect on time, transience, and even find inspiration—sometimes in the most amusing ways.

Reflecting on Time and Transience

Watching those who are returning home makes you keenly aware of the fleeting nature of every journey. They have closed a chapter, reached a destination, and are now on their way back, while you stand at the threshold of your own adventure. Their faces tell stories of experiences, culinary delights, and cultural discoveries, but also of the bittersweet realization that time is always limited.

Yet, this transience is not something to mourn. On the contrary, it is precisely what gives value to the moments ahead. Without an ending, nothing would truly be precious. By acknowledging that your own vacation will eventually come to an end, you can make a conscious effort to savor it fully from the very beginning. The time ahead is a gift, waiting to be unwrapped.

The Psychology of Perspective Shifts

The sight of returning travelers can also encourage you to shift your perspective. Imagine yourself at the end of your trip—what memories will you want to take home? What experiences will you regret not having? This shift in perspective is a valuable exercise, helping you focus on what truly matters.

Thinking about those who are now reminiscing about their travels, replaying their best moments in their minds, reminds you that your own journey is yet to be written. This thought can serve as motivation to embrace every opportunity, to step out of your comfort zone, and to immerse yourself in the beauty of the present moment. The perspective of a returning traveler teaches you to experience your vacation with a conscious and open mind.

Planning Through Inspiration

Returning travelers do not only provide emotional reflection—they also offer practical inspiration. Their body language, their luggage filled with souvenirs, and sometimes even snippets of overheard conversations reveal how they experienced their journey. You might see someone animatedly describing an extraordinary museum they visited, or notice the scent of exotic spices drifting from a bag filled with treasures from a distant market. These small observations can help shape your own journey or add unexpected elements to it. Perhaps you overhear someone raving about a secluded cove they discovered, inspiring you to seek out hidden gems rather than just the well-known sites. Or maybe you notice someone expressing regret about not allowing enough time for relaxation, reminding you to balance adventure with moments of rest. Returning travelers are like living guidebooks, their stories offering valuable insight to help make your own trip even more memorable.

The Humor in Returning Home

Of course, there are also moments when returning travelers bring a smile to your face. You might see someone struggling to reorganize an overstuffed suitcase, trying to fit in a mountain of souvenirs while frantically searching for their travel documents. Or perhaps you witness a family hurriedly navigating the arrivals hall, their arms overloaded with bags, debating loudly about how they will fit everything into their car.

These little scenes serve as a reminder that travel is not only about idyllic moments but also about the small, chaotic, and often hilarious mishaps along the way. They offer a lighthearted perspective on the minor inconveniences of travel—after all, the best travel stories often come from the unexpected, sometimes absurd moments that were frustrating at the time but later become the most entertaining anecdotes.

The Meaning of Returning Home

Returning from a trip is more than just physically going home—it is a transition. Returning travelers exist in an in-between state, where the memories of their vacation are still fresh, but the reality of everyday life is beginning to resurface. Their expressions often reflect a mixture of fulfillment and nostalgia, and their behavior reveals how deeply travel experiences continue to resonate even after the journey has ended. The significance of returning home lies in recognizing how travel enriches life. The impressions gathered, the perspectives gained, and the personal growth experienced during a trip extend far beyond its duration. They change the way we see the world and ourselves. Keeping this in mind allows you to approach your own journey with greater mindfulness, ensuring that your vacation becomes a foundation for lasting memories rather than just a temporary escape.

Travel as a Cycle

Seeing returning travelers also serves as a reminder that travel is a cycle. Every adventure has a beginning, a peak, and an end. But an ending does not mean that the value of a journey is lost—quite the opposite. The return home is often the moment when we truly recognize how much our experiences have shaped us. By understanding that your vacation is also part of this cycle, you can not only appreciate it more fully while it lasts but also accept its conclusion with gratitude rather than sadness. Each phase—from packing your suitcase to stepping back into everyday life—is part of a greater story, one that is uniquely yours to create.

Finding Inspiration in the Magic of Travel

The encounter with returning travelers is more than just a passing moment at the airport. They invite you to reflect on time and transience, to shift your perspective, and to find inspiration in their stories. Their experiences and emotions can help you shape your own journey with greater awareness and appreciation for the beauty of the present moment.

Whether as a source of inspiration, a symbol of life's fleeting nature, or a humorous reminder of travel's little dramas—returning travelers are a part of the magic that makes travel so special. They remind you that every vacation is an opportunity to rediscover the world, create lasting memories, and evolve as a person. And when the time comes for you to return home, you may find yourself inspiring someone else who is just beginning their journey—thus continuing the cycle of travel and discovery.

Hiking along the Spanish coast,

with the sparkling sea before you and the warm sun

at your back, you feel pure zest for life.

Celebrate the Moment

The Art of the Here and Now

The magic of travel begins the moment you arrive. After months of anticipation, careful planning, and eager daydreams, the long-awaited destination is no longer just a place on a map. It is real, alive with movement, sound, and energy. The air feels different, the light falls in new ways, and every breath is filled with the awareness that this is finally happening. But experiencing a destination fully requires more than just being physically present. It requires a shift in mindset, an intentional slowing down, and a willingness to surrender to the moment rather than rushing toward the next.

Savoring the First Steps

The first steps in a new place are always electric. The hum of an unfamiliar city, the scent of fresh bread wafting from a bakery, the warm breeze brushing against your skin—all these sensations become part of the first impression. There is an undeniable temptation to see everything at once, to dive headfirst into exploration, to tick off every landmark as quickly as possible. But travel is not about accumulating sights. It is about immersing yourself in the world around you, noticing the details, and allowing each moment to unfold naturally.

Stepping out of the airport and into the streets of Spain, the transition from traveler to explorer begins. The first meal, whether it is a quick stop at a bustling tapas bar or a long, slow lunch in a quiet courtyard, sets the rhythm for the trip. The first sip of coffee, the first exchange with a local, the first time hearing Spanish conversations swirl around you—each experience layers upon the next, anchoring you in the present.

The Art of Slowing Down

The art of slowing down is the secret to truly absorbing a place. In a world that constantly demands speed, travel is an opportunity to rebel against that urgency. It is an invitation to walk instead of rush, to listen instead of just hear, to observe instead of simply look. Sitting at a café without a phone, watching the way the locals interact, how they gesture with their hands, how they linger over their meals without checking the time, offers more insight into Spanish culture than any guidebook ever could.

Every city, every village, every hidden corner has a rhythm of its own. Madrid hums with the pulse of a capital city, where grand boulevards meet centuries-old taverns, where art and history intertwine seamlessly with modern life. Barcelona dances between the eccentric and the traditional, Gaudí's architectural dreams standing proudly beside Gothic alleyways and lively markets. Seville moves to the slow, steady beat of flamenco, a city that invites you to embrace both its elegance and its raw passion. Granada is a whisper of history, where the Alhambra's intricate carvings and lush gardens speak of centuries past, and where time seems to pause just long enough to let you catch your breath.

Experiencing a Destination Beyond Sightseeing

To live in the moment means not only witnessing these places but feeling them. It means walking without a destination, letting curiosity dictate the route. It means stopping to admire a street musician's performance instead of hurrying past. It means tasting food without rushing through a meal, letting each bite tell its story. A slice of jamón ibérico melting on the tongue, the deep richness of a glass of Rioja, the crisp crunch of freshly baked churros dipped in warm chocolate—these are not just flavors. They are experiences, rooted in tradition, crafted with care, meant to be savored.

There is a profound beauty in unplanned moments. Some of the most treasured memories happen when you least expect them—an unexpected conversation with a friendly stranger, a spontaneous detour leading to a breathtaking view, the sudden realization that you have fallen in love with a city simply by being in it. When plans are too rigid, these moments have no space to appear. Leaving room for the unknown allows for magic to happen.

Resisting the Urge to Capture Everything

The greatest challenge in modern travel is resisting the urge to document everything rather than simply experiencing it. The desire to capture every moment, to share it instantly, to ensure it is preserved forever, sometimes steals the joy of the present. There is nothing wrong with taking photos, with writing down impressions, with wanting to remember. But the most vivid memories are not those seen through a screen. They are the ones fully lived—the laughter shared with a stranger in a tiny café, the feeling of standing in the middle of an ancient plaza, the echo of footsteps in a quiet cathedral.

Letting Go of Expectations

Living in the moment also means letting go of expectations. No trip ever unfolds exactly as imagined. A sudden rainstorm might change the day's plans, a famous attraction might be more crowded than hoped, a highly recommended restaurant might not live up to the dream. But sometimes, the moments that happen instead are better than anything that could have been planned. A rainy afternoon might lead to the discovery of a hidden bookstore filled with treasures. A crowded landmark might push you to explore a quieter, more authentic corner of the city. A missed reservation might result in stumbling upon a tiny, family-run restaurant where the food is made with love and care.

Stretching Time Through Presence

Time moves differently when you are traveling. Days feel longer, filled with more experiences, emotions, and discoveries than usual. But they also slip away faster than expected, leaving only the memories behind. The best way to honor the experience is to be fully in it. To wake up each morning with a sense of gratitude for where you are. To walk through each day with eyes wide open, ready to embrace whatever comes. To end each evening with the satisfaction of knowing that nothing was taken for granted.

Spain teaches the art of presence through its way of life. It is in the slow afternoons where locals gather with friends, unhurried and content. It is in the tradition of sobremesa, where conversations stretch long after the meal is finished. It is in the passionate performances of flamenco dancers, lost in the rhythm, in the emotion, in the raw expression of the present moment. It is in the way people greet each other with warmth, in the way they celebrate life through festivals, food, and music.

Embracing the Now

To truly travel is to let go of the future, to step fully into the now. It is to walk through a city not just with your feet, but with your heart open. It is to embrace the feeling of waking up without a schedule, of wandering without a purpose, of allowing each moment to shape itself rather than forcing it into a plan. It is to be fully alive in a place that is new, unfamiliar, and endlessly fascinating.

As the journey unfolds, there will be countless moments to capture, to reflect on, to cherish. But the most important thing is to live them first. To take a deep breath and feel the warmth of the Spanish sun. To let the sound of a bustling market wash over you. To watch the way light changes over a historic building as the day turns to evening. To allow yourself the simple, yet profound joy of being exactly where you are, exactly as you are.

The Magic of Standing Still

Travel is not just about movement. It is about presence. It is about slowing down long enough to truly see, to truly feel, to truly be. The world moves fast, but when you stand still in the middle of it, when you give yourself permission to be fully immersed in the moment, that is where the magic happens. That is where Spain, and every journey that follows, will leave its deepest imprint—not just on your memory, but on your soul.

In Spain, time moves more slowly
because life here is shaped not by haste,
but by enjoyment.

Extend the Vacation

Playing with Time

Vacations have a way of slipping through the fingers like sand. One moment, the journey is just beginning, the suitcase still neatly packed, the air filled with anticipation. Then, almost without warning, the final days approach, the once-endless stretch of time suddenly feeling too brief. Yet time is not as rigid as it seems. It bends with perception, stretching in moments of deep awareness and rushing in times of routine. The secret to making a vacation feel longer is not in changing the number of days but in changing how each one is experienced. By shifting attention, slowing down, and adopting simple strategies, it is possible to make every hour feel fuller, every experience richer, and every memory more lasting.

Breaking Free from Autopilot

The first key to elongating a vacation is to break free from autopilot. At home, time often vanishes in a blur of repeated patterns. Mornings follow a predictable rhythm, meals are eaten without much thought, and evenings disappear into a haze of screens and routine. Travel, on the other hand, disrupts this predictability, placing you in an environment where everything is new. The more engaged the mind is, the longer time feels. This is why childhood summers seemed to last forever—because everything was fresh, every experience required attention, every day held something undiscovered. By consciously perceiving each moment rather than allowing it to blend into the next, the vacation stretches, becoming something deeper and more immersive.

Creating Daily Rituals for Awareness

One of the simplest ways to slow down time is to create small daily rituals. These rituals serve as anchors, moments of presence that ground the day and keep it from slipping away unnoticed. A slow morning coffee on a balcony, watching the world wake up. A late-afternoon stroll through unfamiliar streets, pausing to take in the colors of the setting sun. A nightly reflection, perhaps with a journal, recounting the day's experiences before sleep. These small, intentional pauses allow the mind to register the passage of time more clearly, preventing the days from blending into one another.

The Magic of Waking Up Early

Waking up early, even occasionally, is another way to create the illusion of a longer trip. The quiet stillness of early morning, when the streets are empty and the world is just beginning to stir, holds a different kind of magic. A walk along the beach before the crowds arrive, the sound of waves uninterrupted by conversation. A visit to a plaza where shopkeepers are setting up for the day, the scent of fresh bread drifting from bakeries. The sensation of being awake before the city fully comes to life creates the feeling of stealing extra hours, of adding secret moments to the day that would otherwise be missed.

Introducing Deliberate Delays

Another powerful technique to stretch time is to introduce small delays before starting an activity. Instead of immediately diving into the next experience, pausing for just ten minutes to absorb the moment creates a sense of spaciousness. Before stepping into the sea, before entering a museum, before taking the first sip of a drink, telling yourself, "Okay, in ten minutes," and then fully experiencing those ten minutes shifts perception. It allows the mind to anticipate, to observe, to build the moment before it happens. Sitting on the sand, listening to the waves, feeling the warmth of the sun, watching the footprints disappear with the tide—these details might otherwise be lost in the eagerness to rush into the water. The same applies before a meal, before a major sightseeing experience, before anything significant. The anticipation adds depth, giving the moment a weight that makes it feel more permanent.

Engaging the Senses to Deepen Experiences

Time also slows when the senses are engaged. The more detailed and layered an experience is, the more space it takes up in memory. Instead of simply tasting a dish, noticing its textures, its layers of flavor, the way it changes with each bite. Instead of walking past a historic building, stopping to look at the patterns in its stonework, the small imperfections that tell its story. Instead of just hearing a song playing from a street musician's guitar, letting the melody sink in, feeling the way it moves through the air. The more senses are involved, the more fully an experience is absorbed, and the longer it seems to last.

Prioritizing Depth Over Quantity

Slowing down does not mean doing less. It means being present in what is happening. There is a difference between rushing through five activities in a day and truly living through three. The mind retains what it has time to process. Filling every hour with too much can have the opposite effect of making a vacation feel shorter, because experiences blur together when there is no space to absorb them. Giving time to each moment, allowing each experience to settle, creates a greater sense of depth and satisfaction. Balance is key. Planning activities but leaving space for spontaneity ensures that the trip does not feel rigid but also does not slip away unnoticed. It is in these unscheduled moments that some of the most profound experiences happen. Sitting in a park and watching life unfold, getting lost in a neighborhood and stumbling upon a hidden café, stopping to listen to a street performer's song rather than rushing past—all these moments add texture to the trip, making it feel layered and expansive.

Savoring the Last Day

The last day of a vacation often feels like the shortest. There is a sense of finality, a countdown ticking in the background. But even this can be stretched with intention. Instead of treating the last day as a rush to fit everything in, treating it as a slow farewell allows it to hold its own weight. Taking extra care in the final breakfast, savoring the taste of the last meal, pausing to take one last deep breath of the air before leaving—these small acts of awareness mark the ending, making it feel full rather than fleeting.

Preserving Memories Through Reflection

Reflecting throughout the trip also adds to the sense of extended time. Keeping a journal, taking a few moments each evening to write down what stood out, not just in events but in feelings and small observations, solidifies the memories. Looking through photos at the end of each day, selecting just a few favorites rather than letting them pile up unseen, reinforces what was experienced. Talking about the day with a travel companion, sharing thoughts on what felt meaningful, keeps the trip alive even as it is unfolding.

A vacation feels longest when it is truly lived. When each moment is noticed, when time is not taken for granted, when small delays create space for appreciation. It is not about cramming in more but about deepening what is already there. The best trips are not the ones that feel like they flew by in a blur but the ones that feel like they stretched, expanding to hold every detail, every sensation, every breath. And when a trip is lived this way, its echoes remain long after it has ended, woven into memory, a part of life itself.

Mindful moments in Spain are filled with sunshine, salty sea air, warm breezes, and pure joy for life.

Inspiration in Relaxation

Creativity in Escape

Something remarkable happens when you step away from the familiar patterns of daily life. The predictable routines fade into the background, the demands of work and obligations loosen their grip, and suddenly, the mind, so accustomed to constant engagement, begins to expand. A vacation is not just an escape from responsibility. It is an opportunity for renewal, a chance to open up new mental spaces where ideas, dreams, and reflections can surface freely. When the body relaxes, the mind does not merely rest—it begins to create.Many of the world's greatest ideas, innovations, and life-changing decisions have been born not in an office or a structured brainstorming session but in moments of leisure. A walk through unfamiliar streets, the sound of waves crashing against the shore, or the unhurried sip of coffee at a quiet café often sparks thoughts that would never have surfaced in the middle of a busy workday. When people are not actively searching for solutions, the best ones often appear on their own.

How Stepping Away Sparks New Ideas

The brain operates differently in a relaxed state. In everyday life, the mind is occupied with problem-solving, organizing, and reacting to immediate demands. There is little room for creative thinking when attention is constantly pulled in multiple directions.

Travel disrupts these patterns, introducing new environments, new stimuli, and, most importantly, freedom from routine. Without the usual distractions, the mind has space to wander, to connect ideas in unexpected ways, and to find inspiration in places that would otherwise go unnoticed. A new setting also provides fresh input that stimulates creative thinking.

Walking through the streets of a foreign city, observing how people interact, noticing the small details of daily life—these experiences spark curiosity. Seeing an unfamiliar landscape or tasting a dish that has never been tried before engages the senses in ways that trigger new neural connections. Suddenly, the mind is active in a different way, processing the world from a fresh perspective.

This is why so many people return from vacations with newfound energy, ideas, and plans. It is not simply the rest that restores them; it is the change in perspective. Stepping outside the daily routine makes it easier to see what truly matters. The worries that once seemed overwhelming lose their power, and possibilities that once felt out of reach begin to seem attainable. A vacation is not just a temporary escape—it is a reset, a chance to look at life with a fresh set of eyes.

Reflection and Planning Life Directions

When life is filled with obligations, it is easy to fall into patterns without questioning them. Work, relationships, and personal projects move forward at a steady pace, often without much time for reflection. Travel creates a natural pause, offering the opportunity to step back and ask important questions. Am I happy with the path I am on? Is there something I have been avoiding? What would I do if there were no limitations?

These are not always easy questions to answer, but they become clearer when considered in a relaxed state. Sitting by the sea, hiking through nature, or simply watching a foreign city come to life in the morning offers a quiet space for self-reflection. Thoughts that might have been ignored in the rush of daily life suddenly demand attention. With fewer distractions, emotions and desires become more visible, revealing what has been hidden beneath layers of routine.

For some, this might mean realizing that a career change is necessary. For others, it could be the recognition that a long-neglected passion needs to be pursued. Sometimes, it is something as simple as deciding to bring more balance into everyday life. Whatever the realization, travel creates the ideal environment to explore it without external pressure.

A useful way to capture these thoughts is through writing. Keeping a travel journal, not just for documenting places visited but for recording reflections and ideas, turns fleeting moments of insight into something tangible. It does not need to be structured—just a place to collect thoughts, observations, and sudden inspirations. Looking back on these notes later often reveals patterns and recurring themes, providing valuable clues about what truly matters.

A Vacation as the Starting Point for Something New

Some of the most significant life changes begin with a single thought during a vacation. An idea that appears during a quiet moment on a balcony, a conversation with a stranger that sparks a realization, a feeling of clarity that refuses to fade—these moments have the power to set new journeys in motion. Many successful businesses, books, and creative projects have started as a thought formed during a break from routine. The mind, once freed from everyday stress, begins to build something new.

Even if there is no immediate plan for change, a vacation plants seeds. A lingering inspiration, a moment of joy that serves as a reminder of what is important, or a realization that a different way of living is possible—these thoughts stay, even after returning home. The challenge is to carry them forward, to resist falling back into old patterns that bury inspiration under routine.

One way to keep the energy of a vacation alive is to integrate small pieces of it into daily life. If time in Spain reminded you of the joy of long meals and meaningful conversations, finding ways to replicate that at home—whether through shared dinners or setting aside time for connection—keeps that lesson present. If a hike through the mountains revealed the need for more time in nature, making space for outdoor activities even after the trip ends ensures that the inspiration does not fade.

For those who feel a strong pull toward change after a vacation, the next step is to create a plan. Whether it is a new creative project, a career shift, or a decision to simplify life, translating ideas into action prevents them from becoming distant memories. Setting small goals, outlining steps, and keeping reminders of the clarity gained while traveling makes it easier to move forward.

Balancing Relaxation and Creativity

Not every vacation needs to be about deep reflection or major life changes. Sometimes, the best creativity comes not from thinking but from simply being. Allowing time to relax, to absorb without analysis, to enjoy the present moment without searching for meaning is just as important. Creativity often works in the background, forming connections and ideas without conscious effort. The simple act of enjoying a sunset, getting lost in a book, or wandering through a marketplace without a plan provides the space for inspiration to emerge naturally. This balance between relaxation and mental stimulation is what makes vacations such powerful creative breeding grounds. The key is not to force it. Ideas come when they are ready. Sometimes they appear in the middle of a deep conversation over a glass of wine. Sometimes they arrive quietly, during a morning walk along the coast. And sometimes, they take root only after returning home, when the memories of the trip settle into place.

The Lasting Impact of Travel-Inspired Creativity

A vacation is never just a collection of experiences—it is an expansion of perspective. It is an opportunity to see the world, and yourself, in a different way. It is a reminder that life is more than routine, that creativity needs space, and that inspiration is everywhere, waiting to be noticed. The most meaningful trips are the ones that leave something behind. Not just memories, but ideas. Not just relaxation, but transformation. Whether it is a single thought that shifts a mindset, a project that begins to take shape, or a realization that leads to lasting change, travel has the power to ignite something new.

By embracing both stillness and exploration, by allowing the mind to wander freely, and by capturing the inspiration that emerges, a vacation becomes more than just a temporary escape. It becomes a catalyst for growth, a space where creativity flourishes, and a moment where new journeys begin.

Under a palm tree, with a view of the turquoise sea,

the best ideas are born in tranquility.

Experience Vacation Like a Local

Step into a New Role

There is a difference between visiting a place and truly experiencing it. Many travelers see only the surface of a destination, moving through it with the eyes of an outsider, capturing photos but never fully stepping into the rhythm of life. To travel deeply, to feel the essence of a place, requires more than just sightseeing. It demands a shift in mindset—a willingness to slip into the daily life of locals, to observe, to participate, and to momentarily become a part of the world you have stepped into.

Arriving in a new city, it is easy to fall into the patterns of a tourist. The instinct is to check off landmarks, to move from one major attraction to the next, to follow itineraries that have been designed for visitors rather than for those who truly live there. But beyond the guidebooks and the postcard-perfect scenes, there is another way to travel. It begins with curiosity, with a slower pace, with a desire not just to see but to understand.

Daily Rituals: Living the Local Way

One of the simplest ways to embrace the local experience is to adopt the daily rituals of the people who call this place home. In Spain, mornings begin not with rushed coffees in takeaway cups but with quiet moments in cafés, where time stretches, where conversations linger, where a café con leche and a piece of warm toast with olive oil and tomato become more than just breakfast—they become a ritual, a pause before the day begins.

Choosing to start the morning this way, rather than searching for the nearest chain coffee shop, shifts the experience entirely. It is no longer about consuming but about participating, about existing in the moment rather than rushing through it.

Walking through the streets, the best way to experience a city as a local is to observe how life flows. Where do people gather? What are they talking about? How do they move through their day? Sitting on a bench in a park or on a shaded terrace, simply watching the rhythm of the place, reveals more about a destination than any tour ever could. The way elders greet each other with a warm embrace, the way children chase pigeons through a square, the way shopkeepers lean in for deep conversations with their regular customers—these details paint a picture of life beyond tourism.

Becoming Someone New for a While

Allowing yourself to be a different person during the trip is part of stepping into the local way of life. At home, routines define identity. People fall into patterns—work, responsibilities, familiar habits that shape the way they move through the world. But travel is an invitation to shift, to let go of the roles that normally define a person, to embrace a different way of being. If locals take long midday lunches, why not join them? If the city slows down in the late afternoon for siesta, why resist it? If people gather in the streets at night, drinking wine and talking well past midnight, why not become part of that rhythm?

Dressing like a local, speaking even a few words of the language, shopping in the neighborhood markets rather than in souvenir shops—all these small choices contribute to a deeper immersion. It is not about pretending to be someone else but about expanding into a new way of living, if only for a short time. The freedom of travel comes not just from movement but from the permission to step outside of your usual self, to explore not just a new place but a new version of yourself within it.

Letting Go of Home to Fully Arrive

Letting go of daily life completely requires more than just physical distance. The mind, accustomed to responsibilities, often clings to what is familiar. Work emails, news updates, habitual worries—these things do not disappear just because you have stepped onto a plane. But living as a local means allowing yourself to be fully present, to release what exists beyond this moment and to embrace what is right in front of you.

There is a kind of liberation in stepping into another world fully, in disconnecting from what usually demands attention, in surrendering to the rhythm of a different place. Eating when the locals eat, adjusting to their pace of life, engaging in their traditions—it all creates a sense of belonging, even if temporary. And in that belonging, a kind of magic happens. The city ceases to be just a destination and becomes a part of you.

Unexpected Connections: Where the Best Memories Are Made

The greatest memories of travel often come not from the planned experiences but from the unexpected moments of connection. The chat with the elderly man at the market who shares his favorite recipe. The bartender who offers a taste of something off the menu, simply because you showed genuine interest. The woman at the bakery who teaches you how to properly order in Spanish, smiling as she corrects your pronunciation. These are the moments that stay, the moments that transform a trip from a series of sights into an experience of life itself.

Tasting a Country Through Its Food

Food is one of the most intimate ways to connect with a place. While many visitors seek out well-known restaurants, the true flavors of a country are found where locals eat daily. The corner bar with a few small tables, where the owner greets customers by name. The market stalls selling fresh ingredients, where home cooks gather to discuss the best seasonal produce. The family-owned restaurant where the menu is handwritten and changes depending on what was available that morning. Eating as locals eat, trying dishes that are not adjusted for tourists but are simply part of everyday life, is one of the most immersive ways to understand a culture.

Beyond food, embracing the arts, music, and traditions of a place deepens the experience. Attending a local festival, even if it is not widely known, stepping into a music venue where no one speaks your language but everyone shares the same rhythm, visiting an art gallery showcasing regional talent rather than international names—these choices transform the way a place is felt.

Wandering Without a Plan: The Key to Discovery

Leaving behind the need to structure every moment of the trip opens the door to unexpected joys. The best days are often the ones that begin without a strict plan. Wandering without direction, following the streets that look most inviting, stopping at whatever café, bookstore, or plaza feels right in the moment—this is how a place reveals itself naturally. There is an energy to a city that cannot be found in an itinerary. It is found in the way the light hits the buildings in the late afternoon, in the laughter that spills out of a hidden courtyard, in the scent of fresh bread drifting from an open window.

Carrying the Local Mindset Home

A trip is always temporary, but the lessons of living like a local do not have to end with the journey. The mindset—the ability to slow down, to observe, to savor, to embrace a new rhythm—can be carried home. Travel teaches that life does not have to be rushed, that joy is found in small moments, that there is always room to connect more deeply with the world. By stepping into the shoes of locals, even for a short time, the journey becomes more than just a vacation. It becomes a transformation, a reminder that the way we move through life is always a choice.

And when the trip finally ends, when the streets that once felt foreign now feel like home, a part of that place stays within you. The memories do not just belong to the trip. They belong to the person you became while you were there. The one who walked slower, laughed longer, tasted more, listened deeper. The one who, for a brief moment, was not just a visitor but a part of something greater.

In Spain, life is lived with ease, good food is savored, long conversations are enjoyed, and life is celebrated.

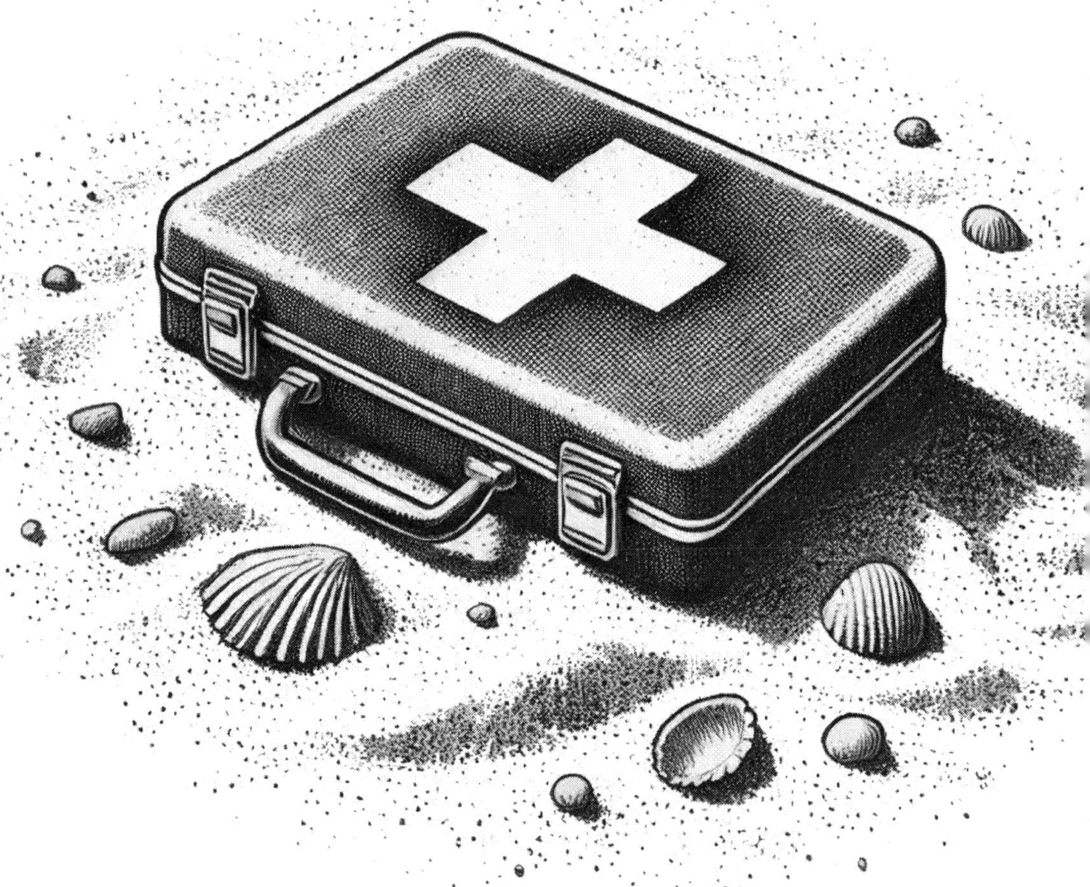

The Vacation-End Emergency Plan

Why the Last Day of Vacation is Just as Beautiful as the First

If you're familiar with my books, you already know that this one important chapter always awaits you at the end. It's particularly close to my heart because it addresses a feeling many of us know all too well: the moment when your vacation slowly begins to wind down. That subtle twinge of sadness as the suitcases come out again and the routine of everyday life starts to appear on the horizon. But don't worry—together, we'll make the most of these final days. The end of your vacation doesn't have to be a reason for melancholy—it can even be a highlight. Every trip, no matter how short or long, has its distinct phases. There's the exciting beginning, the relaxing middle, and, yes, the closing chapter. While the first two phases often feel light and carefree, the end can sometimes be emotionally challenging. But with the right mindset, you can turn this final phase into something special and enjoy those last few days just as much as the first ones.

When the Vacation Starts to Slip Away

You probably know this feeling: Just a few days ago, you felt free and carefree, as if your vacation was an endless oasis of time, sunshine, and relaxation. But suddenly, the days seem to fly by faster. The end feels closer, and thoughts of returning home begin to sneak in. You think back to the moment you arrived and how much time you had ahead of you then. Now, it feels as though the vacation is slipping away in fast-forward.

Let's put a stop to that right here. These kinds of thoughts won't get you anywhere. Instead of losing yourself in a sense of wistfulness, let's focus on what you can control: the present moment. Here and now. And that means fully enjoying every moment until the end of your vacation—without regret, without rushing, and without that "farewell" feeling creeping in.

The Plan – A Clear End Point

Step one in your emergency plan is to establish a clear end point for your vacation. Why? Because so often, we mentally "check out" far too early. Maybe you notice yourself starting to say goodbye to your trip as early as the penultimate day, instead of fully enjoying it. That's a shame because it robs you of precious time. A clear end point ensures you savor every moment up until that time. Decide for yourself when your vacation officially ends. Maybe it's the last dinner, the moment you close your suitcase, or the instant you step onto the plane or into your car. Until then, don't give the idea of "leaving" another thought—it has its proper place and will come soon enough. You'll find it's much easier to truly enjoy the time before then when you're not preoccupied with the end.

The Last Day Is Just as Special as the First

Many of us are guilty of treating the last day of a vacation as a "farewell day," which often feels bittersweet. But why should it? The last day of your vacation is just as valuable as the first. You still have 24 hours to fill with joy, experiences, and relaxation. A simple shift in perspective can help: Instead of viewing the last day as the end, see it as a continuation of your vacation. Enjoy it with the same intensity as the first day. Whether you take one final swim in the ocean, savor a local meal, or wander through the streets one last time—live the day fully and completely in the moment. Remember, we can only ever experience one moment at a time. The last day doesn't have to be a "farewell ceremony" but can instead be another wonderful vacation day.

The Penultimate Day – A Second "Second Day"

The penultimate day often feels like the beginning of the end. But even here, a change in perspective can turn that melancholy into excitement. Treat the penultimate day as a second "second day." Why? Because you still have an entire day ahead of you after this one—a day to do whatever you please, without pressure or deadlines.

Perhaps this is the day to treat yourself to a special highlight: a meal at your favorite restaurant, a visit to a spot you've always wanted to see, or a relaxing afternoon ritual by the beach. The penultimate day doesn't have to mark the start of the end—it's simply another beautiful day to enjoy with intention and joy.

Planning Your Next Vacation

Here's a secret weapon for making the farewell easier: Start planning your next vacation. It might sound strange, but anticipation is a powerful tool for banishing sadness. Where do you want to go next? What destinations are on your bucket list? You don't have to plan every detail, but envisioning a future trip can shift your focus to something positive. Maybe you'll begin a bit of research or jot down a few ideas. These thoughts can lift you out of the "goodbye" mindset and replace it with a smile as you look forward to what's ahead.

Looking Forward to Something at Home

The end of a vacation often feels heavy because the return to everyday life looms like a gray cloud on the horizon. But there are beautiful moments waiting for you at home—you just have to recognize them. Maybe it's a gathering with friends, a delicious meal you've been craving, or a new project you're excited to dive into. It doesn't have to be anything grand—sometimes, it's the little things, like a cozy evening with your favorite movie or a visit to your favorite café, that make the transition easier. These thoughts help you look forward to returning home, rather than dreading it.

Gratitude for the Vacation

Another important step in making the farewell a positive experience is gratitude. Take a moment to reflect on your vacation and recognize all the beautiful experiences you've had. Perhaps you'll write these reflections in a journal or quietly appreciate them to yourself. Gratitude allows you to close your trip with a sense of fulfillment. Instead of focusing on what's ending, you can celebrate the memories you're bringing home with you.

Ending the Vacation with a Smile

Remember, your vacation doesn't end when you leave—it ends when you decide to let it go. And you can do that with a smile. You've enjoyed this time, recharged your batteries, and created wonderful memories. Now it's time to carry those memories with you and look forward to what lies ahead—whether it's your next vacation or the simple joys of everyday life. The farewell doesn't have to be a sad moment. See it as part of your adventure, a bridge to new experiences. And who knows? Maybe your next vacation is already just around the corner. Until then, you have your memories, your anticipation, and the satisfaction of knowing you've savored every moment of your trip to the fullest.

In Spain, you learn to be grateful

for the little moments and to take

things a bit more lightly

- because relaxation is the key

to your vacation happiness.

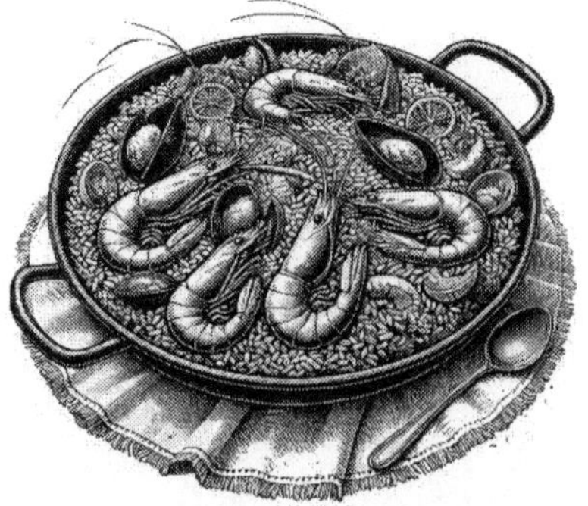

I truly hope this book has sparked your anticipation and excitement! Writing these books is a passion project of mine alongside my main job, and the topic of "anticipation" has fascinated me for years. That's why every bit of feedback means so much to me. Of course, I want everything to be perfect, but creating a book is no easy task. Did you spot any small mistakes? Feel free to let me know – I'm always grateful for suggestions!

If you enjoyed the book, I'd be over the moon to receive a positive review on Amazon. Your support gives me the motivation to keep going and to get even better. Thank you for being part of this journey with me!

Feedback, questions, wishes, and suggestions are always welcome at:

feedback@michaelkissling.com

Kohlenbach 1a, 79183 Waldkirch, Germany

AI tools were used in the creation of this book.

Note: The suggestions and recipes for alcoholic beverages in this book are intended exclusively for readers of legal drinking age. Please enjoy alcohol responsibly.

 ISBN: 979-8-3087-4489-4

Made in the USA
Middletown, DE
10 March 2025